Last Will & Testament

MEMOIR OF A PREACHER IN POETRY AND PROSE

by Cameron Miller

Last Will & Testament: Memoir of a Preacher in Poetry and Prose
Copyright © 2024 Cameron Miller
All Rights Reserved.
Published by Unsolicited Press.
Printed in the United States of America.
First Edition.

No part of this book may be used or reproduced in any manner whatsoever without written permission except in the case of brief quotations embodied in critical articles or reviews.

Attention schools and businesses: for discounted copies on large orders, please contact the publisher directly.

For information contact:
Unsolicited Press
Portland, Oregon
www.unsolicitedpress.com
orders@unsolicitedpress.com
619-354-8005

Cover Design: Kathryn Gerhardt
Editor: Summer Stewart

ISBN: 978-1-963115-12-3

ALSO FROM CAMERON MILLER

The Steam Room Diaries
Thoughtwall Café, Espresso in the Third Decade of Life
Cairn, Poems and Essays

What is required

but to do justice,

love kindness,

and to walk with humility?

                                        The Hebrew Prophet Micah

"Attention is the beginning of devotion."

The American Poet Mary Oliver

There are those whose love has kept me grounded: Katy, for forty years and more, and Anne, Abram, Sarah, and James for as long as they have been alive. There are those in communities of faith who pushed and shoved, pulled and loved, and forever changed me to love greater, deeper, and better. There are those I've found within the subversive preacher community across time and space, most of whom I have never met, yet we share a sacred mystery. There is a community of friends, past and present, still holding hands across six decades. For each and everyone of them I am profoundly grateful. There is even Rabia, who listens to me mutter the words out loud as I write and occasionally raises concerns about the direction of a sermon.

I am also grateful to Unsolicited Press for the support and creativity they have provided me as an author. In particular, I want to thank editors, Summer and Ava for making this better.

To all of you: Thank you, thank you.

CONTENTS

MEMORY FIELD   17

PREACHER
- THE DANCE BETWEEN GRIEF AND GRATITUDE   23
- CONFESSION: I AM A PREACHER   29
- A PREACHER'S LAMENT   37
- CONFESSION: SUBVERSIVE PREACHER   41
- THE OBLIGATORY POEM ABOUT A POEM   46
- SHORT STORY: "WINNING IN THE SHADOW OF 9/11"   52

HEARD AS A PASTOR
- ESSAY: "ACTS OF LOVE"   81
- THE TRANSITIVE NATURE OF "WHY"   84

TRUST   88
- SHORT STORY: "COMMUNITY"   91

DREAMS
- CONFESSION: "ODE TO KARL"   103

MASSACRE AT DAWN	108
"REM"	110
THE WOUNDED ANIMAL SPEAKS	114
AT THE BOTTOM OF MY HEART	117
ALONE	120
SHORT STORY: "THE DESOLATION" —A JESUS TALE BASED ON MARK 1:9-13	120

LIVING

ESSAY: "A 'GOOD' LIFE"	128
BROWN LEAF	133
COME OF AGE	138
CHANGE	141
ESSAY: "SLAP ME!"	144

HEALING

CONFESSION: "VIRGINIA"	150
CONFUSED BY THE PRESENCE OF ABSENCE AND THE EMPTINESS OF HOPE	156
MULTIVERSE	160
FOR DECLAN AND WESLEY	163
BEFORE I CIRCLE THE DRAIN	164

TORCHLIGHT TOURS OF THE PSYCHE	166

SPIRITUALITY

ESSAY: "A CHRISTIAN MANIFESTO"	172
THE LORD OF GENOCIDE	179
PARABLE	180
PATHETIC LORD	182
RESIST!	184
MERCY	188
PSALM 139	190
A PRAYER ON BEHALF OF THOSE WHO SPEAK IN ORDER TO HEAR THEMSELVES THINK (EXTROVERTS)	191
ESSAY: "GOD"	195
SHORT STORY: "THE CONVERSATION"	199

AWED BY THE ORDINARY SACRED

ESSAY: "AUTUMN"	216
I WONDER	219
INVERSE WISDOM	221
TWO POETS WRITING	223
TO THE POEM SURGEONS	225

WHEN I AM DEAD AND GONE	227
YOGI FRIEND	231
THE COLORS!	232
MOONLIGHT SONATA AND AUGUST RAIN	234
ESSAY: "SNOW THIEF"	235
THE GOD WHO EATS BLACK HOLES FOR A SNACK	237

PARTING (NOT LAST) WORDS

ESSAY: "WORDS WIGGLE AND MEANING IS SLIPPERY"	251
ESSAY: "IS IT A WONDERFUL LIFE?"	255
ESSAY: "THE PROMISE OF OUR HOPE"	258
ESSAY: "A WORD MEDITATION FOR THANKSGIVING"	260
ESSAY: "THE CIRCLE BE UNBROKEN"	264
FUNERAL	267

ACKNOWLEDGMENT	277
THE BACK STORY	278

Last Will
& Testament

MEMOIR OF A PREACHER IN POETRY AND PROSE

Memory Field

Have you ever sat in silence in a room full of people, most of which you do not know, as they listen to the labored breathing of the person everyone is either staring at, or studiously trying not to see? In a colorless hospital room, I mean, where machines with little lights whoosh and beep a serenade to the life ever-so-slowly seeping away?

Perhaps you know what it is like to slather your thumb with frankincense-infused oil while holding an hours-old infant and catching the glimmer of her parent's tearful joy as you make the sign of the cross on her forehead? Perhaps you've done the same with an infant that has recently died?

Have you greeted people at the door as they leave worship and received gratitude from someone because the sermon you preached resonated in the quiet stillness of their heart? But then, the very next person in line berates you for what you said from the pulpit?

Surely, you have had the experience of suddenly realizing you just spent four hours—which felt like five minutes—midwifing the birth of ancient wisdom into contemporary sermon text? No, perhaps not. But really, why should you have done such things?

Being a preacher is a real niche experience. By saying preacher I include pastor as well, since they are two roles normally performed by the same person. I prefer "preacher" because, in my practice, it is the relationship established through preaching every week that lays the foundation for the more intimate, but occasional, pastoral role. Besides, I also like that a preacher sounds somewhat less polite and cultured than pastor or priest.

I am an Episcopal preacher, which means almost nothing to most people. It is my brand not my limit. I am a Christian before I am an Episcopalian, and a child of God before I am anything else. While I practice Christian spirituality and am a teacher of Christian sacred wisdom, I am not limited to those expressions either. God and spiritual wisdom defy definition and human limitation, so why should we keep ourselves confined to home?

I do not know when *old* is, but I may be living on the banks of that Rubicon. Over the decades, I have covered a lot of ground, which is not some kind of boast, but rather, a looking back as the son of a man who lived and died in the same town he was born in. Across that distance, I have had the privilege of sharing in the lives of thousands. That means being present to and sharing with intimacy a withering array of extreme joys and tragedies: from sudden infant death to suicide and spontaneous healing, to depression and anxiety, to baptism and marriage, and copious conflicts and resolutions. Nobody asked for it, but due to all of those experiences I have something to share that will resonate with others.

This may be the last will and testament, but hopefully not the final word. God willing, I will keep writing. But this is as close as I will come to a memoir. Much of what you will read here has a clear autobiographical ringtone and there is no hiding it. In that sense, this is a memoir in poetry and prose lifted from four decades as a preacher. However, if revealing my story was the point, I wouldn't have invited you to read it. Rather, as in preaching, if my own life experience can open something useful for someone else then I will use it. These essays, poems, and short stories are offered in the belief that they host insights and mysteries that may be valuable to someone else. None of this poetry or prose unveils anyone else's story—not even mine completely—but as with any writing, they represent a conglomerate of experiences.

So, as a preacher writing poetry, a poet writing essays, and an essayist writing fiction, I offer you my life's experience in which I invite you to discover your own. In so doing, perhaps you will encounter the ordinary presence of the sacred in the midst of it all. I recommend reading the poems, especially the sermonic poems, out loud (I always read out loud as I write).

Also, the thematic order in which they are placed is only suggestive, so feel free to read them in any order you wish. As always, may the holiness of peace be with you.

Cameron Miller
Finger Lakes, New York

Preacher

The Dance Between Grief and Gratitude

A sermonic poem inspired by...
a Jesus story
a Marie Howe poem
and Finger Lakes poet, Lisa Nichols, eating the sun.

When grief begins
it is anything but ordinary.
It is a trauma
landing
with the force of a horse
sitting down
on its rider.

But eventually
it works its way into the ordinary—"that old grief."

We start talking to the dead person we miss
as if he or she is standing next to us,
and as if it is not weird
that we are talking out loud
to someone who has died.

We just do it
because, well, because
it has become ordinary…

When our heart
finds its place in gratitude,
grief becomes ordinary.

When gratitude
becomes big enough,
or deep enough,
or just plain solid enough,
it holds the grief.
Before the ordinary, grief
holds everything else
including gratitude, so
it isn't ordinary yet.
It is still the dragon
guarding the entrance to our mind and heart
and letting nothing pass
without it first being singed
or outright scorched.

But one day,

the dragon goes missing
and the other things in the cave of our mind
and heart
start interacting with the grief,
and the grief becomes conversational.
And then, if we allow it,
gratitude for the person who has left us
grows and grows and grows
and starts to collect the grief in its arms.
The grief is still there,
but now it is held by gratitude
and becomes—more ordinary.

Then one day,
without warning,
without planning,
we are living again.
It feels odd, at first,
but then gradually, we are thrilled
to be living again.

Can you imagine what it would be like
if we all got to do what Luke says Jesus did?
You know, die

and then walk around living?

Well, if we did that,
then we would all write poetry
like Mary Oliver.

We would walk around
savoring every small thing
we had rarely noticed when we were alive
and we'd just touch it,
or kiss it,
or hold it.
A single blade of grass would be so marvelous
it would make us cry.
A snowflake would take our breath away.
A toad hopping in the grass,
or a worm writhing in the soil,
or the diamonds the sun scatters on the morning waves
would make us swoon.

We would walk around savoring
every small, delicious
molecule of life
just dripping with gratitude.

Thinking about Jesus being like Mary Oliver,
walking around looking
and touching
and oohing and aahing
At every small and delicate thing
that never begged a notice before,
makes me want to try it.

What if, on Monday mornings,
we ogled and savored?
What if we slowly ate the sunrise?
What if we very slowly breathed in
the scent of love?
What if we ran our fingers
along a smooth wood finish
and stuttered helplessly over every grain?
What if we peeled an apple
and sobbed at its clean, simple lines
and stunning colors?

Five minutes.
Only five minutes.
Five minutes once a week

savoring the world as if
we were the dead
given one last chance
to encounter bodily life through gratitude.

Oh, to be Jesus back from the dead
savoring every small thing life has to offer
and getting blown away
by beauty
even on the battlefield of grief.

Maybe that is what resurrection is—
to come to life
in the midst of life
and fall head over heels
in gratitude.

Confession: I am a Preacher

My last night home before leaving for seminary, at the Ponderosa Steak House in Muncie, Indiana, I asked my parents what they thought about my becoming an Episcopal priest. It had occurred to me earlier during the visit that I had never heard them say anything about my decision to enter the seminary.

Understand the context here. It was amazing that I had graduated college. When I was a senior in high school I had decided not to go. Frankly, it would have been difficult for me to be accepted to any college, and looking back, it is a wonder I graduated from high school at all. It is generally agreed upon by those who know me well that I likely have some kind of undiagnosed learning disability, the kind of thing that was never known or measured back then. Then again, there were numerous active ingredients at work in this psycho-social misfit who did poorly in school.

You see, I flunked second semester geometry during my sophomore year. The teacher came to me the week of the final and showed me his attendance record. I had missed exactly half the classes that semester. (In my defense, it was a first period class at 8:15 a.m.). He told me I would have to get a B- on the Final to pass the course. I walked out of the class, liberated from enduring another test. But my sister and her boyfriend badgered me into taking the Final by commiting to helping me cram. Nearly all night we prepped for the test, and I took it first thing that morning. I was stunned by the C+ I scored, but he gave me an F for the course anyway.

That left me having only passed first year Algebra and one semester of geometry. Without my knowledge, my parents signed me up for Advanced Algebra and Trigonometry. What defect of reason made them think I could pass that course is beyond my imagination. By the end of the first semester, I made a deal with the teacher to drop the course if he would let me pass it with a D. Technically, that gave me four semesters of math with passing grades, even though they were in two unfinished subjects. Added to this distinction was when I flunked the fourth semester of Spanish during my second semester of junior year. I did thrive in social studies and art, though.

The SATs were not what they are today, but they were something. I got righteously drunk the night before and mostly filled the little answer bubbles in randomly. So, had I applied to my brother's Alma mater, Princeton, they wouldn't have invited me in. But what did I care? I had my eye on a job working for the Episcopal Diocese in youth ministry. Yet, at the last minute that job did not materialize. I long suspected my dad of back channeling a kill order on that hiring in hopes I would apply to college somewhere. It worked.

It was June 1972. I had graduated from High School, somehow. But applying to college that late?

One of my older sister's former high school buddies raved about the small college in Ohio that she was attending, a hundred-and-fifty-year-old women's college that had just become co-ed. In fact, I learned later, my grandmother went there, ferried from Muncie by canal and carriage. The Western College (for Women until 1972) was looking for men. It was aggressively progressive. They had only written evaluations and no letter grades. It emphasized international education and perspectives. Three hundred and fifty students, mostly women, in a beautiful, wooded campus at the edge of Oxford, Ohio. They were happy to accept me. Remember, this was in June! Even with the more relaxed college admissions process of those days, this seems miraculous to me now.

I loved Western, but even so, at the end of my first semester I was warned that I was close to flunking out, despite not receiving letter grades. Then a sociology professor convinced me to take a speed-reading course (I tested at a third grade reading level) and harassed me over and over with repetitive writing assignments until I learned to write competently enough to pass my courses. Where else would, or could, that have happened?

During my second year, Western announced it was bankrupt

and closing. I had declared as a philosophy major, which was something my parents didn't remark on either. I had learned that both my dad and my brother received their lowest college grades in philosophy, which made my interest and competency in it all the more rewarding. I leaned into Chinese philosophy, and the professor with whom I had taken most of my courses encouraged me to go to the University of Delhi and study Buddhism. My parents did remark on that idea.

Circling back to that night at Ponderosa Steak House, the fact that I had now graduated from Skidmore College with a remarkably acceptable grade point average and a degree in philosophy, was a galaxy away from where I had begun. I suspected that my parents were quietly beside themselves that I hadn't ended up derelict someplace with someone calling in the middle of the night to report a tragic ending. But there we were at Ponderosa, silently eating our steak and baked potatoes with me flying to Boston the next day.

"Well?" I asked.

"Well, what?" my dad responded, looking up.

"Well, what do you think about my joining the seminary. Neither of you have said anything about it. What do you really think?"

I was a glutton for punishment. Historically my mom was critical to a fault, at least with me. Our relationship was a bloody one, in which pain had been inflicted in both directions for years. At the time, I claimed the privilege of being her victim, and only later did I come to recognize the contributions I made to the situation. My dad was painfully passive and an extreme introvert. It was almost always a mistake for me to ask them how they felt or what they thought about something in which I was deeply invested.

Silence followed my inquiry until finally my dad said, "Well, it is alright, I guess. I would never want to be one."

"Yes, it is fine," my mother chimed in, "but I would never want to marry one."

That was it. Forever.

I am not sure I ever heard either one of them express pride or dismay at me becoming an Episcopal priest. But then, I never heard either one of my parents say anything when I told them I was in recovery from alcoholism. Perhaps, for those two children of Victorians, these are things one simply does not talk about?

Now, some four decades later, I no longer wonder what my parents would think, but I am struggling to discern what I think about my profession and how I exercised it. It took ten years for me to get comfortable wearing a clerical collar in public, which I did for about the first two decades. Since then, I only wear a clerical collar when professionally necessary, i.e., in worship or at the hospital. Like many professions, both its substance and its status has changed radically since I entered into it. I am embarrassed to say I became a priest for ontological reasons—to be an agent of God in some peculiar way, and with very little understanding or interest in the profession itself. Somehow, like graduating from high school and college, I wandered my way through it all anyway.

I once asked my dad what he would do if he could do it all over again, and after some reflection he said he would be a farmer. I never thought my dad wore his profession comfortably, he was an attorney, but it was easy to imagine him as a farmer. There is no other profession for which I can close my eyes and say, "Yep, I should have been one of those." I am a preacher, a preacher who writes.

A preacher is not something I set out to be or even knew was a thing. "Preacher" evokes the image of sweaty bible-thumping jerks who pronounce judgment on everyone that doesn't fit into their own narrow view of the world. I am not one of those. But I won't define it for you either, at least not here at the beginning. If you keep reading this memoir naming what a preacher is, if indeed it is a thing, is a question you can enter and struggle with as I do.

Looking back on my professional life from this little catbird's seat, I see that I have been a preacher and likely will continue to be one even when I no longer have a physical pulpit. In fact, I wandered away from the typical limitations of the pulpit quite some time ago even while remaining in churches. (One of the things I value most about The Episcopal Church which ordained me, is its lack of guardrails).

I am less certain that I have been a priest, let alone a good priest, as the institution of the Church defines it. I have done priestly things and often found meaning in them—indeed, I have been deeply humbled by them. But I am not the purveyor of comfort for those with a defined faith, nor am I a sacramentalist dispensing forgiveness, grace, and certainty. Rather, I am a poet who preaches about the whirlwind we live in and the whispers sometimes heard in the stillness at the eye of the chaos and in the wind.

I am a preacher that picks at the scabs that form over our most basic assumptions and uses a jackhammer to find the next one buried underneath. I am a preacher and use words to dig deeper and metaphors and memories to break through to the next assumption buried beneath that one. I am a preacher, and I know that God is manifest in the cloud of unknowing and mystery unspoken—the so-called thin places where the veil between the Holy and us is most shear, unnerving, disorienting, dissonant, and shocking, rather than saccharine sweet and cherub cuddly. I am a preacher and point toward the places we are most vulnerable, then play on those strings with a poetry that aims to hit a nerve. I am a preacher and hold up the exquisite presence of the sacred hiding in plain sight at our fingertips and feet. Whether I am in the pulpit or confessional, teaching or facilitating a meeting, by a bedside or hovering over the bread and wine at the altar, I am a preacher.

It is what I am more than what I do, and I have been it for most of my life now. I am a preacher.

A PREACHER'S LAMENT

My soul is heavy,
a sluice swift with doubt.
    It is this trace I trod.
Followed,
year after year,
congregation
after congregation,
questioned, yet still taken.

I am a harbinger of sorrow
   to those who do not
      cannot
will not
adapt.

How many have left
these many congregations
lo these many years?
It is this burning,
    penetrating charism

with which I have been anointed.
How many, O Lord,
how many?

I bring misery
    and am pestilence,
        to those who wish to sing the old songs,
    say the old prayers,
        hear the old versions,
        speak the old tongue
with the same old cadence.

I am a contagion of horror,
threatening preservation
    and conservation
        of things sacred—
though my only desire
has been to open
    and share them.

New people come.
Renewed energy is born of this brand,
but replacement and restoration
does not heal the weariness

from those whose faith feels injured—
    mistreated and abused.

They are lovely to someone,
those who grimace
and gnash their teeth.
To those they love or like
they may even smile, but
    I disappoint
    and hurt them all.

For what?
Slightly altered worship—
something shoved kicking and screaming
two centimeters
when it needs to be shoved a yard
or two hundred?

Surely, dear G-d,
    this is too small a thing
to spill blood
and anguish over?
Isn't there more
    and better work to be done?

Something greater
to have spent these years—
 this life—upon?

Confession: Subversive Preacher

"They call you 'prophet.' Did you know that?"

It was a chance encounter in Starbucks, a place I went to get a gift card for someone who preferred it to my coffee haunt. Now, awkwardly for me, standing in the fake hip of the tidy blond wood cafe, she said she had things she wanted to tell me before I left town. She had wondered if she would get the chance, she said, and smiled. The last thing she said was, "They call you 'prophet.' Did you know that?"

It hung there echoing inside me like ocean waves clawing at sand. I knew what that meant thirty years ago, but I have since unlearned it. Forty years ago, I even aspired to be it and would have thought being coupled with the word was a zenith. Now the whole concept of being prophetic is an exquisite poem of impossible beauty I can read but never write, and which I dare not read aloud for fear I would do it poorly.

Months earlier, when I first announced I would be leaving the congregation to go to another one, someone else looked me in the eyes and said, "You taught us how to live again. We had forgotten. You know how the world is, how it is today? We needed to learn how to live again, and we didn't even know it."

The warm tears on her face when she said it somehow made me paralyzed. *But I don't know!* I shouted inside. *How could I do what I don't know?*

(I break here to say this is not a catalog of lauds and sugar I received over the years. In fact, plenty of people have left congregations I served, angry and enraged or simply disappointed that I wasn't what they expected. There are a host of witnesses who would testify against me in the court of church, so please don't get the wrong idea here.)

Anyway, the encounter in Starbucks took me back to another time thirty years before. Oops, longer even. On retreat with congregational leaders, the outside facilitator asked the participants about my preaching themes. He prepped them by saying preachers only have so many sermons in them, and that most sermons are variations on a few core themes. What, he queried, were my themes? To my amazement and chagrin, the members of the church board peppered the newsprint with themes and phrases, some of which seemed only vaguely familiar.

They listen? I was in shock.

Almost immediately I made plans to register for The College of Preachers in Washington, D.C. Somehow, I had made it through three years of seminary and two years of internship without ever believing that anyone listened. The fact that sermons mattered was big news to me.

What I know now, which I did not know then, is that preaching can be powerful. It can also be dull, boring, trite, and manipulative, too. But there is a kind of preaching that changes lives, and sometimes, on the lips and lives of people like The Rev. Martin Luther King, Jr. and Archbishop Oscar Romero, preaching changes the world. The cosmos is full of small, seemingly insignificant elements that are overlooked and undervalued, but nonetheless work magic over time and change the nature of the ecosystem within which they are embedded. Now I know preaching can be like that and I live in awe and reverence of it.

Do I believe I am a prophet, or that I taught anyone how to live again? I cannot afford to believe such things. But I do believe that preaching is subversive, and that if the preacher brings his or her own life to it, it can be powerful. If the preacher has the courage and trust to open up his or her own life to the sermon, and then allow the sermon to use the good, the bad, and the ugly of the preacher's life for the good of the sermon, then things happen that are downright difficult to explain. I do not mean unwarranted or sloppy self-disclosures that are inappropriately intimate for the setting, rather, for the preacher to submit his or her own life to the sermon being preached in the same way the congregation is being asked to do.

When preaching is authentic like that, and deeply rooted in a relationship with both the text and the community, then the preacher and the community are changed over time in ways that none of them could expect. It is subversive to the preacher as much, if not more than to the community.

I can tell you this: There is a moment in the midst of some preaching when something happens between the preacher and the congregation akin to lovers locked into one another's gaze. It is when both parties suddenly recognize the truth of what is being shared and stripped of ego, it connects the hearts of each in a way that didn't exist just a moment before. It lasts a nanosecond and then is gone.

When there are enough of those moments, when preacher and congregation stand naked together before the same truth, then a powerful bond is formed. It is always a mutual process, never one-sided.

For as long as I can remember, I have closed my eyes and prayed silently before delivering each sermon, asking that God's presence be known, not mine; for God's word and wisdom to be heard, not mine. While I routinely get tangled up and in the way of what I prayed for, sometimes something else happens too. Like I said, the effect of preaching is cumulative, never just one big moment. Subversive preaching requires the elements of time, disguised repetition, opening the things that matter, and the accumulation of shared moments of vulnerability.

"Prophet" was a case of mistaken identity. Perhaps just a subversive preacher.

THE OBLIGATORY POEM ABOUT A POEM

A poem can't change the world
so is it then
too small a thing?

Poems aplenty, sure,
sounding anguished tones
over changes already wrought:
after the fact poems,
Johnny-come-lately poems,
poems grieving
or celebrating
giants of courage
and momentous changes.
But a poem voicing power?
A river of words
overflowing the banks of language
and leaping into the currents of time and space
coercing change?
No such poem
ever.

Sermons and novels and books of ideas
can make the case
for cracking the shell
that opened the universe
to transfigured time
and space.
Maybe even a play? *Hmm*—probably not.

Words have been known
to change the world
when uttered well
upon the tongue,
or through the pen
and poured
upon the hearts of enough—
or just the right few—
people?

But a poem
distilled down the narrow passageway
of a single life
one at a time
is too small a thing

to push the river.

The poem,

a mere droplet

landing in water

weeping into the current

is gone.

We should aspire to more,

better,

greater things

than a poem.

And yet this.

Essay: "Psst, your pet doesn't know your name"

My dog is a show-off. Every morning when I roll out my yoga mat and begin a stretching and exercise routine, she saunters over to perform a pluperfect Downward Facing Dog. She usually does it parallel to whichever direction I am facing so that I can't miss her exquisite form.

"Yes," I said to her the other day, "but that is the only pose you can do." Then I showed her my best Pigeon pose, looked over my shoulder and said, "try that." She flopped down and feigned sleep.

Despite how that sounds, I don't anthropomorphize my dog. That's a big word that turns out to be important. "Anthropomorphize" means to ascribe human characteristics to things that are not human.

I recognize my dog does not know what I think. Nor does she understand English. Even the words she does recognize have more to do with the way I say them than with linguistic comprehension. That is not to say she is without keen senses with which to recognize my mood and what I want from her. She does, just not the same ones humans capitalize on.

It is easy to project all kinds of human characteristics and emotions onto our pets. They are companions to us in times both painful and joyous, and so we form a powerful bond. We can have deep relationships with animals, especially those with whom we live, but we need not drift into imagining they are like us or that we understand them.

There are trees I have known with which I formed a bond. I even gave some of them names. But to then ascribe human attributes to an organism which cannot reciprocate would be dangerous to my mental health.

We have famously anthropomorphized God, too. Think of the Sistine Chapel. Michelangelo's "Creation of Adam" on its ceiling gives God a Zeus-like image that appears in form to be the senior version of the younger Adam. It comes from the Judeo-Christian idea of Imago Dei, which assumes humans were created in the image of God. It is a sneaky way of anthropomorphizing the Creator by working backwards from us to "Him" or "Her." The logic is if we were made in God's image, then God must be like us.

Ascribing human attributes to things that are not human is hazardous. While it does allow us to feel more kindly toward whatever we are projecting ourselves onto, doing so also prevents us from embracing that creature's true nature. When they disappoint us—as they always will—we get all kinds of angry. How many people have rejected faith because God didn't do for them what they thought God should have done, based on the assumption that God is supposed to act like we do?

It shows greater honor to other life and elements of the Earth when we know and greet them as they truly are, rather than erroneously casting them in our own image. Taking time to learn the true nature of dogs, cats, deer, trees, lake, birds, plants, or whatever, allows us to have more authentic relationships with them— which means a safer existence for both.

Short Story: "Winning in the Shadow of 9/11"

"I don't know how those people ever know if they've won. Do they win? Ever?"

That was all he said. These were the only words Jonathan's Yale Law School father ever spoke to his son about the son's decision to go to seminary. He said it while peering down his nose as if toward a bad smell. The young man waited for his father to say more about the decision, a decision which was earth-shattering and life changing for the twenty-four-year-old. But over the ten years that passed prior to his father's death, nothing more was said about it.

An important trial kept the successful attorney from attending his son's graduation from seminary three years after that underwhelming response. Another important trial kept him from attending the ordination ceremony that followed six months later. But after Divinity School and landing a plumb job as lead pastor in a large socially prominent congregation, establishing himself years ahead of his cohort, even Jonathan wasn't sure how to recognize or measure a win. Still, he was pretty sure he hadn't put up any points on his father's scorecard.

Now, ten years out of seminary and three years after his father stopped winning, defeated by a fatal heart attack under silk sheets in the bed of a mistress, it was Thursday morning, September 13, 2001, and the young minister felt desperate to score points. All the stately old churches of the mainline Protestant traditions would see a record number of people in their pews, and it was urgent that some of his members gave him a "10."

This was the moment he and his young colleagues had all been waiting for, when church would mean something again. September 11th was the shadow to which they all felt the urgency to bring light.

Gnarly old Jacob Higbie, the pastor who mentored Jonathan for two years after seminary, used to bark, "Preaching is no job for a grown man." Yet, the old man was the best preacher Jonathan had ever known; anyone could easily tell he changed lives with mere words. On any given Sunday, tears rolled down one man's cheek as a smile of serenity curled another's lips. The fact that there was an abundance of men sitting out there in the pews with the still more generous numbers of women and children, was itself a testament that the old man could preach. The ghost of old Higbie was haunting him now, reminding him of the old man's prowess in preaching but also the relentless integrity his mentor possessed.

Higbie did not let his greatness go to his head; he kept himself humble by humiliating the station of preaching, reducing it to a ridiculous anachronism. But now, as the clouds of asbestos dust and smoldering black plastic smoke blew in the Manhattan winds above what was the World Trade Center, everyone, anywhere in the leadership of a congregation, could feel the pregnancy of the moment for Christianity—heck, for religion itself. For Jonathan it was a moment to score points even though on that Tuesday morning, when the world watched in rapt horror as CNN replayed the event over and over and over, Jonathan had refused to be bothered.

He had been huddled with his church finance team pouring over two decades of budgets and endowment data in order to understand the financial profile of his new congregation. They were there to develop a blueprint for a solid financial future. When his secretary knocked, opened the door and apologized for the interruption, he treated the news that an airplane had crashed into the twin towers with exasperation. Just another incident like the one in Florida where some idiot had flown a Piper Cub into a vacant apartment building. He shooed her away and kept the volunteers corralled; he had been trying for six weeks to get those volunteers to give two hours of uninterrupted time to this project.

Even after full knowledge of what had happened penetrated his resistance, he was deeply suspicious of how it would be used by the new Republican administration as well as news media. While he was not blind to the suffering unfolding before the nation and world, he could feel a dark anger and the voice of theological invective rising in him at the same time. As often happened inside Jonathan, a spring of anger bubbled and rose above the banks of his empathy. He was constantly sandbagging the brink to keep it from flooding over.

Images of Firefighters and Police running into the flaming towers to what would be their certain deaths showered the airwaves, hailing them as heroes. He could see for himself it was true how selfless they had been in their attempts to save others. Still, suspicion and resentment toward authority was a deep aquifer within him. He could also see and hear the political machinery revving up the engines of divide-and-conquer. He could see and hear spokespersons for local churches and not-for-profit organizations making self-aggrandizing claims to warm up their fundraising motors. The dark angels that hide in the shadows of bigotry and xenophobia were barking now about Muslims in America. Jonathan was hypersensitive to these ghouls in the body politic.

But just then, on Thursday morning, he felt the horrendous weight of expectation to say something soothing on Sunday. Even the national news media was saying that people would flock in great numbers to sanctuaries across the nation to hear a message of hope, feel assured, and find meaning in the terrible event that had shaken the nation. A local newspaper reporter had called him, taking an inventory of "special events being offered to mark this great national tragedy."

Gag. Jonathan hated expectations, especially when they were handed out by profit-sucking organizations or anyone in authority that thought they knew what he should do. People would arrive at St. Columba's expecting the American flag to unfurl in the Light of Christ, but he had removed the American flag from the sanctuary his first week on the job. He still bore the bruises of that campaign and harbored resentment for it as well. They would arrive unable and unwilling to separate the religion of nationalism from the religion of Christianity, and his meticulous efforts to untangle them, especially in so raw an atmosphere of national grief and fear, would infuriate those that came for red meat.

This was a hazardous opportunity, a dangerously teachable moment.

The time had arrived to score big in a way even his father would have understood. Yet, there he sat staring at a blank white page on the computer monitor. "Damn it," he cursed, "don't freeze me out." He was speaking to his muse, or maybe to God.

***

The Rev. Jonathan D. Samuels paced in and out of his church office, his secretary nonplussed by this most anxious presence. Ruth had been the church secretary longer than the pastor had been alive; she wasn't about to let Jonathan's skittishness make her anxious.

"Ruth," Jonathan announced more than asked, "are people going to expect me to wax patriotic?"

Ruth studied the young man's face before answering. It was a pleasant face and she was certain that the soft angular features of it, both beautiful and manly at the same time, gave this pastor his advantage with the congregation. Two predecessors ago, The Rev. Terrell Pugh, had a face populated with red, rough looking divots that required onlookers to drink from their deep well of compassion in order to look as they listened to him speak. Never mind that The Rev. Pugh was brilliant and as faithful as the days on a calendar, his lack of even a moderate attractiveness limited the sway he could hold with his people.

Too early, Ruth thought, to know how this pastor's tenure would end. That handsome face and his creamy voice gave Jonathan a head start, but what kind of a steward would he be of this advantage God had entrusted to him?

"People love their country, Jonathan, that's a fact. You can't be running down America if you want people to listen to what you have to say about Jesus."

That was pretty much what he expected her to say, and it was exactly what he was afraid of—what he already knew. Still, he was hoping for something better.

"Doggone it, Ruth" he snapped, though he would rather have said "Shit, America has nothing to do with Jesus and vice versa. How are we ever going to get to truth if we have to hide behind Christmas lights?"

She knew he wasn't really talking to her, so she didn't answer and went back to playing whack-a-mole with the music texts she was trying to insert in the Sunday bulletin, using a new desktop publishing software. Every time Jonathan changed his mind and edited or added prayers, which was often, it moved the music around and that threw everything else off. She thought Jonathan needed a younger, more computer competent person to be his secretary, but she wasn't ready to retire yet. He would just have to deal with it, she thought.

Jonathan stared off into space before pacing back into his office.

His preaching routine had been thrown off by the unfortunate intervention of Jihadists and Sunday morning was fast approaching. His old mentor, Pastor Higbie, had tutored him in the wisdom of not waiting for inspiration. "If you wait for inspiration every sermon will be a Saturday Night Special and no damn good."

So, the old man had insisted the young preacher under his tutelage follow his own tried and true method. First, on Sunday afternoon, before going home from church, read the bible readings appointed for the next Sunday. Next, spend a little time each day meditating upon them, praying over them, and studying them. Finally, come Thursday, get up early and start writing and don't stop for anything—not even bathroom or lunch—until the sermon is done. Jonathan had been doing this for almost a decade now and in all that time his congregations had only been stuck with one or two Saturday Night Specials.

Thursday had now come and gone. It was Friday afternoon and he had been trying to write his post-September 11th sermon since Thursday morning, that unmistakable feeling of powerlessness was crawling up the inside of his arteries.

Lord Jesus Christ, he said to himself as he inhaled, and *have mercy on me*, as he exhaled. In and out, in and out.

He sat there in his cushioned office chair inhaling the words slowly and exhaling the words slowly, over and over and over again. This almost always worked. He could feel his heart slow down. He imagined his blood decelerating to a trickle. Soon there would be room for the Holy Spirit to enter and speak. It might be a big idea, or a single word, or even a small syllable, but whatever form it took it would be enough. *Lord Jesus Christ…have mercy on me.*

Nothing.

Not one word, image, thought, or sound. There was nothing but his own breath and soon the return of his rapidly beating heart. This was not fair. Time was escaping and he had other things to do. He couldn't spend Saturday trying to come up with something. He was coaching his youngest daughter's basketball team at the community center in the morning and at night he had to attend a celebratory dinner for his wife's best friend who was pregnant after having tried for five years. In between was a long list of errands and chores he already knew weren't getting done.

He threw in the towel.

It was Friday after three p.m. and he could feel the total emptiness of whatever sealed chamber it was that normally granted sermons. Jonathan did not know where they came from or how they got to him, but sooner or later the sermons arrived, and he wrote them down. He had never tried to describe it to anyone. He wouldn't even if he could. It would sound far more mystical and spookier than it felt to him. To him it was just a matter of opening some spigot inside and keeping up with what flowed. There was rarely even much editing unless he lost focus while trying to capture what was revealed. It remained an off-balanced spectacle that he never really felt in control of.

As a matter of fact, it would often happen that Jonathan didn't fully know what he was saying until he preached it. In the pulpit, suddenly and out of nowhere, he would recognize the full depth and breadth of what he was standing up there mouthing. The awe of that experience never diminished and always humbled him. It could even make him feel stupid at times.

Friday afternoons were fruitless. He would come into the office and putter around, but he was always inefficient. Most of the time, by mid-day on Thursday, after writing the sermon, he was so tired that his productivity slowed to a trickle. By the time the sermon was written there wasn't much left. Normally, when the sermon was finished on Thursday, he wouldn't look at it again until Saturday about an hour before bed. Then he read it through, made small edits, and printed it for delivery.

He wrote out his sermons differently than anyone he knew. Instead of paragraph form, he wrote them as he spoke them. They looked like long free-form poems the way he formatted them in 18-point font. It allowed him to read the text without looking like he was reading it. Truth be told, he was ashamed he had to write his sermons out, but when he didn't awkward words, fuzzy ideas, and jumbled thoughts fell from his mouth. As much as he admired preachers who could wander the aisle and talk without notes, he learned early on that he was a writer who preached as much as he was a preacher that wrote.

Pastor Higbie confirmed Jonathan's limited sense of discretion after Jonathan once preached about "Jesus eating with scumbags and whores." Higbie pointed out at least a dozen offhanded words <u>and</u> phrases Jonathan had used that were deeply offensive to his middle-class audience. Jonathan simply was not good on his feet. Whatever course language was in his head passed through his lips. Thus, he honed his writing skills so that the often poetic and eloquent text hid the actual crude and inelegant state of his inner voice.

But now, the sacred process that usually worked had run dry. Perhaps, he was dry. Was it him? No, he was jazzed by the moment that had arrived, and was jumping internally for this opportunity to score points so rarely available to him. It was the muse or God being impetuous. Jonathan wasn't sure which it was nor who was currently to blame, but he left the office sulking.

***

Some days, coaching fifth grade girls' basketball was sweet as it gets, other days it was miserable. September 15th was beyond miserable. He knew it would be when his daughter, Hannah, was awakened and immediately started wailing, refusing to play basketball. With too little coffee and almost no breakfast, he had dragged her whiny ass to the community center where she walked around with slumped shoulders and fish lips. Then there was the little redheaded girl that stood at his heels throughout the game yipping, "Put me in coach, I'm ready coach."

They lost by twenty-seven points and all the girls but one were inconsolable. Hannah was simply apathetic.

***

On the day of the sermon, he dreaded seeing Miriam P. Showorthy walk in with her ivory-handled cane. There were any number of people he hoped wouldn't show, like Alistair Weeble with his serpentine smile and the sickly sweet, perfumed Janet Nelson with an equally sickening sweet persona. But it was Miriam he dreaded most, perhaps even feared.

She was a Brahmin with an air of authority few dared chAlange. This armor was her greatest defense but when some nabob did contradict her, her eyes glared and her leather lips pinched, and silence enveloped the room with a magical force sucking all life right out of the moment.

Jonathan knew what he had found to say would not please Miriam P. Showorthy and she would have the support of a third of the congregation—mostly Republicans, but really any of the professional class with a high sense of propriety. They would all be conscious of what was being preached that day at their church, and in the private clubs around town it would be compared to what the other High Steeple pastors had said from their pulpits.

Jonathan suddenly realized that was how people like his father, the ones that still went to church, kept score. Not only did he have to win for himself, but he also had to win for those who paid his salary and supported the ministries of St. Columba's. He felt a bead of sweat leave his armpit and roll down his ribs.

Jonathan was always nervous before preaching a sermon. He could not remember ever ascending the steps of a pulpit without his stomach quivering and his lips suddenly drying out. He used to think it was an odd pathology but then began to associate it with the other thing that happened when he preached. It could be sixty-two degrees in the massive stone chancel, which in the winter it often was, but midway through the sermon Jonathan would be sweating. As soon as he stopped preaching, he would stop sweating. The sweating rarely began right away, rather only at that moment in the sermon when he connected to whatever it was he connected with. Whatever it was, it had a way of finding Jonathan when he least expected it. That was the impetuous nature of it—it was in charge, Jonathan wasn't.

Sometimes the sweating would start and he wouldn't recognize it until he was soaking wet. All of a sudden, he would realize his shirt was damp, and then would be left wondering at what point it started. But for Jonathan, he was better off looking back than being acutely aware in the moment, otherwise, he would get distracted and lose his way.

That was another reason he used a text. Jonathan was an extrovert's extrovert, which meant he was easily distracted by the reactions of people around him. He had learned to create a visual fog so that he could look out at the congregation while he was preaching or celebrating Communion but not see anyone in particular. He could look right into the congregation without seeing Miriam P. Showorthy in the third pew on the right or the woman with the white linen blouse open at the top who had recently been attending. Often people would ask him, "Who was that sitting in the middle section toward the back?" But Jonathan could only list people he had greeted at the door that morning.

Today he was already nervous when processing up the center aisle behind the acolyte with the smaller of the two processional crosses (the larger one in front leading the choir). He knew Miriam P. Showorthy and her cohort would already have conjured up blame for what had happened in Manhattan and were looking for him to affirm their worldview from the pulpit. But he also knew that most of the people sitting in the pews were more like Lindsey Russell, the bird-thin nurse that worked the night shift so she could be available to take her six-year-old son to the bus and meet him when school was out. Lindsey would arrive hoping to hear something that made sense of the terror, something she knew instinctively but couldn't put her finger on and would never hear on television. Jonathan talked with dozens of people each week like Lindsey who were never as certain about the meaning of events as Miriam P. Showorthy, and who were strengthened by grappling with the questions and buoyed to hear others grapple too.

Jonathan watched his scuffed black shoes poking out from under his white robe as he climbed the four steps into the massive mahogany pulpit jutting out in mid-air twenty feet above the congregation. The nave held nearly a thousand when the balcony was open and that day it was. The singing was stronger than usual, and he could hear human voices above the locomotive volume of the organ as Fritz pulled out all the stops, and was manically playing "A Mighty Fortress Is Our God."

Jonathan was out of body, watching himself cross the chancel as he climbed the pulpit. He allowed himself a peek at the congregation but regretted the indulgence immediately. In addition to the flash of hundreds of faces he knew were expectant, each with a different expectation, one face appeared like a lighthouse lantern amidst all the rest. It was Miriam P. Showorthy, scowling already.

"Let us pray."

He paused. Jonathan never prayed in sermons, but today was different and it had a dual purpose.

"Abba.

Ganesh.

Allah.

Adonai.

Holy, holy, holy, Lord God of hosts.

Open our hearts and minds in this moment of grief.

We are not Christians, Jews, Muslims, or Hindus today –

we are your people and the works of your hands. Amen."

Here Jonathan paused for a long time, but because everyone present was full of emotion it did not seem long or empty, just quiet. He looked out, yet saw no one as he employed the screen of fog trick he had learned to manage attacks upon his focus. He felt himself taking a slow deep breath without a conscious command, inhaling slowly through his nose and exhaling equally slowly through his mouth. It was exactly what he did during meditation and prayer hundreds if not thousands of times each week.

"It is as if our entire nation of two hundred
and seventy-five million people

were a small Vermont town

gathered around the square, together,

across time and space.

We have been standing together

under the shadow of our two greatest fears:

death and evil.

Since Tuesday,
we have been stumbling through the days –
stumbling as we do
when we are of two minds:

one that sees the work or tasks or errands
in front of us,

and the other that drifts away
to an indistinct murkiness

where thoughts and ideas
are never quite completed.

For those of us
who have lost close personal friends
and loved ones,

we recognize this fog
as the aftershock of grief.

When grief barges in
we are condemned to that strange
double-exposure

in which we watch ourselves
drift through the mundane tasks of living

and wonder why everything around us
is going on as if nothing has happened.

It is a hazy discombobulation

that comes over those
who are in the shock of death—
a kind of disassociation
that allows us to function,
but just barely.

We are all in grief today,
a deep personal grief
whether or not we knew anyone now resting
in that mass grave once known as 'The World'.

Every one of us, young and old,
has lost plenty and we are feeling it.
You can name the litany of losses
as well as I can:
sense of security,
innocence,
freedom,
hope…and on and on and on."

Someone sobbed audibly and Jonathan was momentarily distracted. Then several people coughed or cleared their throats and Jean Tyson's baby made his customary loud sucking noises as he nursed.

On a normal Sunday there would be plenty of commotion to cover the silence now grounding the sanctuary—baby noises, toddlers wiggling or even running in the aisle, or in winter the clanging pipes as the heat churned on. But today was just quiet; any and every motion or sound seemed loud, but not loud enough to penetrate the strange pall of silence encompassing all.

"But we have looked Evil in the eye.
We are the once innocent Luke Skywalker
feeling small
in the shadow of a towering Darth Vader
because this week we abruptly
encountered real evil.
Human evil.

The capacity to hate,
destroy,
to even take pleasure or pride
in the decimation of God-given life
is fearsome to behold.
It makes all of us feel small and vulnerable.

It is, of course, all around us all the time,
in more defuse ways,
and within each one of us too.

But to stand naked in front of a towering evil
so intensely focused that it destroys in seconds
what was one of our most impregnable fortresses,
is to know that evil is abroad
and to anticipate that it may get even bigger
and more intimate than we fear.

For me,
the most chilling moment this week
came when I realized,
in addition to the multitudes who were shocked
and angered by what happened,
there were also thousands or more
who cheered
at the news of our deaths.
Around the world
there were people celebrating
the death of thousands of us.
They are not the people who did this,
and they are likely good and loving neighbors
to their own friends and family.
All such people
that celebrated what we grieve,
are people just like us.
Somehow,

they and we
are not a collective 'us'
and the source of that separation
seems too hot to grasp."

Karl Mellenger's sister was a mess, and Karl was pretty sure no amount of therapy and no treatment program would fix her. But no matter, he was supposed to drive with her and her poor husband down to The Pines Recovery Center later that afternoon. The whole world was going to hell in a hand basket—the stock market was probably about to crumble, and he wouldn't get much of a bonus this year because of it, and as always, his little sister Sandy had found a way to keep herself the center of the family's attention.

Jonathan Samuels is an idiot, Mellenger thought, as he watched the preacher praying in the name of other gods as if it was going to create a Kumbaya moment in the pews. What the stupid bastard didn't understand is that money rules the world not theology.

That was "Mellenger's Rule" and he was going to have to break the news to Samuels. *Evil?* Karl chuckled to himself so loud his wife gave him the Clint Eastwood stare. *If it weren't for America and the US Treasury there would be a whole heck of a lot more evil in the world*, Mellenger retorted to himself.

Karl looked around and saw the Social Worker and her husband crying and heard the people he didn't know behind him sniffling, and he had a direct line of vision so he could see old Miriam P. Showorthy up there fuming. *How long is Samuels going to talk today anyway?*

"Surely, there is so much about us

as a people

that they do not know –

our goodness, generosity, and kindness.

If we shared a boat together,

them and us,

or a kitchen table,

or a backyard,

we would surely come to care about one another.

Even so, I am left wondering

what is it they know about us

that we do not know about ourselves?

We cut such a wide swath in the world,

we Americans,

and we leave a wake

where we didn't even know

the water was troubled.

What is it we should know

about ourselves
that could possibly evoke joy
at the sight of our death?

The deaths we can handle, we have to.
Death must always be handled—
endured, recovered from,
no matter how it is wrought.
Knowing them
and them knowing us,
that is an even greater chAlange.
Knowing one another
is finally the only weapon we have
against evil."

Suddenly, Jonathan wondered how the congregation was receiving his sermon. A worm of panic wiggled up his stomach and got loose in his chest. He needed to be present in the moment, not allowing his damaged ego to run free.

"To bridge the distance
between them and us
is our one and only weapon against evil.
This is not a religious or ethnic conflict,
it is a human one.

Evil is the gravitational power
of a life lived in a descending orbit
centered around the Self.

Once we have allowed our Self
to be the center of our universe,
and we have been captured
by its centripetal force,
we are capable of ever escalating
acts of evil
because all other life
is here to serve our purpose.

So, if we want to do battle with evil
we better get ready to cross boundaries,
open the gates of our soul…"

Just then, Cabot Scott, a two-and-a-half-year-old whose head was much too big for his unstable little bandy legs, popped out of the second to the last pew in the back and ran for it up the center aisle toward the pulpit. As if his life depended on it, Cabot waddled in high gear toward the front with his magnificently lithe auburn-headed mom in hot pursuit. A few heads turned to see what the commotion was, but Jonathan didn't react, and most eyes remained riveted toward the front.

Cabot's mom did a miraculous job chasing down the toddler, scooping him up, and sliding into the back pew without a great deal of commotion. Cabot gave up his freedom without a peep.

"Before Tuesday it was not in my mind to say,
but after the bombing of the World Trade Center
it seems obvious:
spiritual community
around a radically open table
is our best
if not our only hope
to stem the tide of violence.

Of course, no community is perfect and we will never have the capacity
to eliminate evil,
but radical openness
will keep us from falling too deeply
into a descending orbit
around our self-interest.
Radical openness
around a common table
will put us in tension with each other;
it will be uncomfortable

and it will stretch us farther

than we would ever ask to be stretched.

But isn't that what we need?

Isn't that where we encounter

God most powerfully?

What makes ordinary community

spiritual

is the uniquely powerful

presence of God

that takes place

when we practice radical openness

around a common table."

The rest of the sermon swirled around the same drain, drawing on the story from Luke appointed for that day by the New Revised Lectionary. It wasn't the eloquent locomotive transporting all present into deeper self-knowledge and understanding that he had dreamed of, but it was all he had. It was all the muse, or God, gave him. He wanted more and he knew the Miriam P. Showorthys of his world wanted better too, but that is all they got from him. He had learned from failure more than once, that when the hose runs dry it is better to go thirsty than fill up on something that isn't clean.

The firestorm began that Sunday afternoon with phone calls between the elite members of the congregation, and it carried on at bridge tables in the woman's club later that week. It was widely agreed upon in that circle of the church that Jonathan had not spoken of the terrible event in New York, meaning he had not waved the flag and engaged in anti-Islamic vitriol. Jonathan had not measured up to the competition and therefore embarrassed the august patrons of St. Columba's. Not only did he not win, but he hadn't even placed.

Jonathan came to discover that the social workers and the teachers, the stay-at-home moms and the guy with the severe limp whose name no one knew, had heard a sermon that day about September 11, 2001, and it had helped them find an order for their thoughts and feelings.

The man with the severe limp whose name no one knew, looked him in the eyes as they shook hands on the way out, and said, "Thank you for your refreshing authenticity at a time when it is easier to go along with the mainstream narrative."

"You're welcome," was all Jonathan could say. But in the days ahead he would hold onto those words when Miriam P. Showorthy made his life miserable.

Heard as a Pastor

Essay: "Acts of Love"

At a family-related party in a bar, a woman with her teenage daughter introduced herself and thanked me for saving her brother's life. The daughter chimed in, adding how important her uncle is to her and thanking me as well. Now, that is an introduction that will get my attention.

They were referring to events that happened a decade previously, fresh and wet for them, but for me I needed to squint down the long sleeve of memory in order to see what and who they were talking about. I did not save his life, of course. It was his willingness to acknowledge a power greater than himself that led to his sobriety, and his willingness to enter the community of other alcoholics and do the work he needed to do. All I did was tell him what I noticed.

I know the feeling that someone has saved your life though, even if only because they said something.

Some years ago, I went to the doctor for a routine physical. Quite soon after entering the room he asked me how I was sleeping. That question led to a forty-five-minute conversation that centered on the fact that I had become a workaholic, obsessed with fulfilling a task that was impossible for me to redeem. As I look back on it now, it began an intervention that would slowly evolve over several years to save my life. At the end of the conversation, I asked my doctor why he had asked how I was sleeping. "You look tired," is all he said.

It was more than the words, of course, the insurance company probably only paid him for seven minutes of his time with me. In the time-management reviews of the medical practice that month, he probably received demerits for taking too long with a patient on a routine annual check-up. In fact, that doctor left the practice soon after, and went into some other field of medicine. I remain forever grateful to him.

Most of the time it is very small things that make a difference—it's the accumulation of many small things that finally creates transformations.

In our glampy, celebrity-studded, everything-hyped media culture we can get fooled into thinking it is the big things, the famous people, and the power-lunches that do things that change the world. But it is ordinary people doing the small things that lead to transformation. Small words, spoken at just the right time or said just the right way, with our hearts and minds opened at precisely the right moment for small words to enter, can make all the difference.

Small acts of love, even teeny tiny ones, add up.

Small acts of love added to small acts of love, accumulating over time, pushing the balance toward transformation, is how big changes for the better happen. Often, we only see the sum total of all those acts, not each one itself. But the physics of change is built upon the diminutive rather than the big and glitzy. Every cultural and political movement in history that finally transformed the body politic, were granular and built to a swell over time until reaching the tipping point of change. Every grain is significant to the outcome.

It is easy to become cynical and hopeless in our time, confronted as we are by an onslaught of information weighted heavily with the dramatic, traumatic, and awful. But it is our willingness to continue these small acts of love, one step at a time, that will lead us to a new and better world.

THE TRANSITIVE NATURE OF "WHY"

I (When why is emptied of curiosity)

Why am I alive?
It is a wail, an echo,
a sorrowful look
bereft of words—why am I still here?

Whispered from a pew,
beneath stained glass,
even when washed in rainbow droplets of light,

or muttered from a downward face
told to the urine-soaked linoleum
of a nursing home
that is no home.

It is that despair
from those who have run out
of money

friends

capacity

but also, even from those who never will.

None of them can fathom

why they have not run out of time.

My father felt it.

His eyes wrinkled and his nose

crinkled exposing a mix of confusion

and despair

when he tried to say it.

To say it

was more intimate

than he knew how to be,

but his wife and friends had hit the exit.

He could not hear,

and he should not have driven,

and it hurt him to walk.

So, I know how old too old is.

It is the moment

at whatever age we are

when we do not know
what we are living for.

When life is no more than
one day in front of the other
strung together by breathing
with no vision of greater purpose—
no expectation of joy—
when life has been let out of living.

Breathing and sensing
in pursuit of more breathing and sensing,
is life without living.

II (When why becomes a statement)

Why is my son dead!
Why did this happen to me!
Why doesn't God do anything to help!

In florescent rooms,
surrounded by beeps and swooshing machines,
with humans tethered to life by tubes,
"why" becomes

a statement—an indictment
even.

III (When why becomes what)

What do you mean
you don't know what happens
when we die?

It was never a question I expected
to be asked—
not even in young days
when I thought mysteries
were for unfolding
and God was for knowing.

It was a question
I answered only once
never to make that mistake again.

TRUST

Once
a voice changed me
to trust

G-d.

The problem,
the voice said without using any words,

was not
the black hole
within the border of my anxiety,

it was the absence of trust
at the beginning of my faith.

Years after the voice spoke
without using words,
a thin veil dissolved in the river of my tears.
Then, I could see.

I had tried using

G-d

an aphrodisiac,
a palliative,
an obliterating anodyne
to eradicate
the terror cells
inside.

Then one day,
which arrived over and over and over again,
I learned all the questions
to which I most wanted answers,
could be asked
but never revealed.

Live with it,

        the voice said without words.
How?
I asked with words:
sometimes loud words,

sometimes bitter
hostile words,
sometimes ugly words.

Trust,

the voice said.

Just trust.

Short Story: "Community"

The old woman looked at him with strained seriousness, no hint of a smile except in her pale blue eyes. He noticed the deep imprint of crow's feet spreading out from the corners of her almond-shaped eyes even without her smiling. Then, mechanically, he bowed his head. As his chin moved downward each cervical vertebrae complained about the unfamiliar gesture.

It felt awkward standing between two women he didn't know, in a posture of humility that wasn't familiar, receiving something he didn't even know that he wanted—or what it really was. The intimacy felt like a closet.

But there he was, in a two-hundred-year-old neo-gothic church, in the corner, in front of a giant marble baptismal font, which was elevated on a step-up pedestal from which the two women looked down at him. The other old woman, fat and sweaty, placed her hands gently upon his head. He felt her squeeze ever so slightly and it made him picture the helmet they place on the condemned for electrification. He chastised himself for the thought.

It was a sunny Sunday outside but inside the church it was dark. The thick blue, red, yellow, and green stained-glass windows lowered the intensity of the sun while the overhead chandeliers cast yellow light that spread out and barely touched the pews below.

He didn't belong here. He felt that in his body. This was a place of softness. Surrounded by hard stone and dark wood, and the scent of old books, it did not feel like his world, or any world he believed in. There was a quietness syncopated by singing, people that should not be singing bellowing out hymns with abandon, seemingly unselfconscious about it. Where was their shame? There was an absence of shame in this place. It felt uncomfortable, as if the guardrails had been removed and he was walking along a hazardous precipice.

Yet, there he was leaning over so a squat, round lady could could reach the top of his head and cup her hands over it. The other old lady now fingering his forehead with a fragrant oil in the shape of a cross and whispering up close to his face, "God, lover of souls, heal Curtis with your holy, life-giving Spirit. Infuse him with your love and surround him with your grace."

That was all. Time for him to move on so the next person could receive what he just did. Whatever it was. It was something though, he could feel it.

A burning sensation right in the middle of his chest. Exactly where the melanoma had penetrated his body was burning. He tried to get ahold of himself and shake it off, but he was also hyper aware there were people all around who might be looking. He always imagined people looking at him—up to him, for him, through him. He was an important person, the Chairman of the Board for a Fortune 500 company. Earlier he had been a "Fixer," the guy who came in and cleaned up other, lesser men's messes. People feared him and were in awe of him and he knew they watched as he walked by.

But it was unclear to him if anyone in that place was looking. It was a strange feeling, but he thought that maybe no one cared who he was, at least not when they were all in that dark place. One of the mysteries he had encountered there was that identities changed in that place, or more accurately, were lost. It was a life raft in which status and accomplishment all disappeared and only the ability to all row together mattered. It was part of the awkwardness for him.

He returned to his pew and slid in next to his wife who was praying and didn't look up. He sat there Godsmacked, that burning sensation moving into his shoulders and down into his groin. It moved through meridians down his legs to his feet, and around his shoulders down his spine. Instead of reacting to it, he just sat there receiving it, not knowing what it was or if it was okay. *Is this what a heart attack feels like?* he wondered for a split second. Then, for one of the few times in his life, he lost track of his thoughts. He lost control of his thinking and simply sat there, holding in a light he could see and feel within himself.

When the sensation passed and he opened his eyes, he was aware of his wife looking at him. She had seen something too.

She had seen her husband, a man who split wood to relax and whose face never had a soft expression on it, appear loosened and calm. She even felt the tension between them evaporate. In that moment, something was changed about him, and she both wanted and feared to ask what had happened.

He turned his head slowly toward her and in a tone she had rarely heard from him, he told her he was healed. He was sure of it. The cancer that had penetrated his chest and metastasized in his lungs, was gone. He didn't expound on it, he just said it with a matter of fact certainty.

She was as powerful among her own peers as he was among his. She had enormous wealth of her own and was an art dealer of some notability. She was also practical and took nothing for granted. As they later tried to process what had happened, she insisted that he allow his doctors to pass judgement on this new certainty that he was a healed man.

He had only been given a short time to live, so he had retired, leaving a position of great power and prestige to put things in order while he still could. Now, he was well, he was sure of it. His vigor was back, and he was outside every day working the acreage he loved amidst the horse farms that surround his island of wooded and grass land. He could fly fish in the brook at the edge of his property, hay, ride the tractor to cut the grass in the mowed sections, and split wood. But now he wanted to make a difference in that church.

He lived twenty-two miles out in exurbia, and that historic stone building sat in the downtown of the even older struggling city. His drivenness was now focused on how to pay God back, or whatever it was that had given him a second chance. He had never been a churchgoer, attending at Christmas with his wife if she insisted the family all go together. It didn't make sense to him before. He couldn't figure out how those guys up there in the gowns could set goals and complete them. How did men in their situations know when they had won or lost? What would they even win? There seemed to be no end goal, no way to measure. The whole thing made him uncomfortable and irritated.

Now he wanted to fix it. He went to the minister and told him that he wanted to make a difference. Did their finances need fixing? Were they getting enough in pledges from the congregation? What was the long-term plan and how would they prepare to make it through the next downturn or recession? The minister appointed him to a committee that frustrated him immediately.

He was used to having power and wielding it to get things done. But that wasn't how this system worked. In fact, he couldn't really understand what the system was and what, if anything, made it work. The minister talked about community and consensus, and this set the man's teeth on edge. That wasn't how the world really worked, but he recognized he was the outsider here and needed to learn. After all, he had been healed in order to do something special, surely.

His doctors had been amazed that, in fact, there was no longer any sign of the cancer. A complete remission, they said. It was a clean bill of health, though they wanted him to come back every six months for a checkup. The now healed executive and his wife gave credit to the minister, even though the minister had nothing to do with it and confirmed so. But it was the man at the top that got credit for the good results of the organization, so they were sure it was the minister. So they became every week attenders, and both the man and his wife were eager to make their mark upon the church—which they saw as the building more than the community. How could they help the congregation afford the massive building that previous generations had bequeathed to the current generation, a smaller and less affluent cohort than their ancestors?

The minister was not helpful. He was kind and supportive and led a good worship each week, but he didn't seem to understand, or care, about what it would take to properly endow and secure the building. *It was a beautiful monster that would kill them all,* the man thought, *if they didn't figure out how to feed it.* On that, he and the minister agreed.

The minister had become convinced that the building was the problem. The congregation, he realized, associated "Church" with the building. It was the historic structure with forty-foot-high timbers and renowned windows that the people actually belonged to. The organ and paid choir offered a strange kind of concert each week as the soundtrack for the rituals from the red book in their pews. It was birthing a community of intersected lives that the minister wanted to create, and the building was only valuable to him so long as it served that purpose. The man with the healed melanoma slowly began to understand.

The man joined the sandwich-making team that made hundreds of sandwiches each month for the homeless ministry. He stood next to the old lady who had made the sign of the cross on his forehead and came to know her. They laughed and chatted and listened to one another's stories. She in turn asked him to join their Habitat for Humanity team. It was perfect for the man! He could be part of something he could see had a beginning and an end, and he could take part in making it work. In the process he got to know people who worked with their hands for a living. Unbeknownst to most people, he had grown up in a working-class family and the whole thing made him feel like he had come home.

The man slowly eased into life in the congregation, the "community" as the minister called it. He came to care about people and could feel them caring about him. He even came to depend upon that indescribable feeling of being known—the good, the bad, and the ugly—and being cared about anyway. When the old lady was in the hospital, he visited her. When she went home, he made sure she had all the medical equipment she needed to facilitate her own rehabilitation. The fat lady became a pew-mate to him and his wife. It wasn't long until his old colleagues and friends in the business community began to whisper about the man. He'd changed. He openly talked about being healed and about what he was doing at church. It was awkward even, like being around someone who quit drinking.

It wasn't until the third anniversary of the healing that the man was told his cancer was back, and this time with a vengeance. They offered him the possibility of experimental treatment protocols, but the man declined. It was okay this time, he said.

The church was packed for his funeral. Several corporate colleagues and social peers showed up, along with many members of the church and the folks he connected with at Habitat. After a couple of the man's children and a brother offered eulogies, the minister got up to speak.

He told the tale of two men, the one who first arrived at the church and the one who was being buried from it. He told the story the man had told him, about coming to church at the persistent insistence of his wife. They had been facing the grim prospect of his Stage Four cancer diagnosis and she wanted him to get some comfort, she said, even though he said he didn't need it. For her then, she begged. He came. He actually liked the sermon and the music that first week and came back the next. Sitting there as other people went forward for Communion, he noticed the old lady and fat lady at the font, laying hands on people and praying over them. There was a small line that formed as some people left from receiving the bread and wine and went to receive a prayer.

In the bulletin it said they were "prayers of healing, with the laying on of hands," which was some kind of ancient tradition among those people. Without thinking about it, even though he was loath to act impulsively, the man got up while his wife was as at Communion. He went and stood in line. It was a whim by a whimless man. It was an act that changed the man's life, the minister said. The minister went on to tell what the man had learned, as he had told it to the minister.

Later at the reception, as the minister made his way along the smorgasbord of fancy foods, pausing in front of the shrimp cocktail while a jazz combo regaled the crowd, a man with a square face and flat expression approached him. The man was from the corporate world and in a scolding voice told the minister that the man he had described in his sermon was not the man he knew. He was unapologetic when he told the minister in no uncertain terms that he had been wrong about the man changing. He told the minister, people do not change like that. Then the corporate man walked away.

The minister wondered what had been so scary in his sermon. Which of the things he revealed about the dead man had unnerved the detractor so? Then, he remembered that when he had first met the now dead man, soon after his healing, how he wanted to fix the building and fix the church and fix the finances and fix whatever needed fixing.

Then the minister remembered his last conversation with the dead man. The image of serving him Communion filled his thoughts, and the dying man's changed face. *Healing does not always include curing*, the minister thought to himself. Then he smiled as he picked up three jumbo shrimp to put on his crowded plate.

Dreams

Confession: "Ode to Karl"

He was my therapist for five years, off and on. Intermittent instead of constant because I was chickenshit.

I don't know how old Karl was exactly, but I'm guessing he was my senior by at least fifteen years—just enough to almost keep me humble. Plus, he was a Jungian, that oddball strain of therapy that seems to me to be the Masonic Order of psychology. It is not exactly secretive, but it is definitely peculiar and ritualistic. Actually, Jungians are more exotic than Masons, so the better metaphor is from religion: They are mystics in contrast to a monolithic hierarchy looking down from diagnostic thrones.

Karl had been a Baptist minister in his previous life, before studying in Geneva, Switzerland, the Mecca for Jungians. His former profession gave him an uncomfortable degree of insight into my vulnerabilities. He used that weapon sparingly and well.

I have been blessed to have several good counselors and therapists throughout my life, as well as a couple of really fine spiritual directors. Every guide needs a guide, and as Parker Palmer writes, the true work of a leader is his or her own interior work.

The most hazardous leader is one who does not know him or herself well, and who moves reactively to his or her own demons rather than proactively toward a chosen direction. Because I am an intuitive leader more than a linear one—able to see where to go from the place I am standing, but not necessarily the incremental steps to get there—being non-reactive is crucial. Therapists, spiritual directors, and colleague groups are resources that have helped me to lead in my vocation.

Working with Karl turned out to be special. As much as anything, I think, it encouraged me to tune back into my dreams. Jungians love dreams.

I taught myself how to remember dreams when I was a teenager, long before I even knew there was a method for it. Dreams had been an important piece of self-awareness for me even from childhood. But from my mid-thirties until late in my forties, the disrupted sleep of a father with young children separated me from that part of my life. Karl helped me reconnect.

Some nights I am a dream machine and it causes me to miss Karl even more—he had a terrible stroke not long before I moved to Vermont. Working with Karl, then leaving full-time parish ministry and moving, caused my dreams to live closer to the surface. Writing poems did too. But also, when I finished my first novel, I was surprised by a sudden grief over having to say goodbye to those characters who had been living inside me for a year. All of this kept my dreams vivid and lively, and it was a dream that precipitated the changes.

One afternoon in 2012, I woke up startled from a dream. I had been driven to the precipice of change in my life, even losing my grip on all the things that had been most important to me. Karl had helped me acknowledge a deep vein of depression in my life, as well as accumulated and unprocessed grief. Yet, I was struggling, trying not to let go of what I knew and the security it gave me. That afternoon I took a nap with the sun pouring in through my window and warming me on the bed as I slept.

In my dream I was standing before the leaders of my congregation who were trying to get me to understand something I was, nevertheless, not comprehending. It seemed to be a life and death matter and the moment was filled with high emotion. "Open your eyes!" they passionately urged. I hadn't realized that the reason I couldn't understand was that my eyes were closed—in that magical and blurry dream-reality kind of way.

But as hard as I tried, I couldn't open my eyes.

Then, I realized I was hovering on the boundary between wakefulness and sleep, actually trying to open my eyes. My eyes were also halfway between open and closed and twitching back and forth in each direction. When I could finally open them, I knew exactly what I needed to do: leave full-time professional ministry and become a professional writer."

It was so clear and so cogent. It had the authenticity of a God-whisper that I didn't even question, nor have I since. Such trust is rare in my life.

Dreaming did not get any less potent as my ministry profession morphed into a part-time role (and identity), with two successive congregations that were small and single cells, rather than big and complex. Across that same time there was the change in fatherhood as my children expanded their now autonomous lives and my marriage took on the chAlanges of the empty nest. All of these things and more churned the ocean inside.

Today, I wake up on many mornings tuned into a dream, and then try to remember other dreams that played in the theater of my mind that night. I am listening, though not quite as carefully as I might, were I still meeting with Karl. I know now that dreams can be truer than true—the voice of God unfiltered by the haze and distortions of consciousness. But they can also be misleading and wrong, the tantrums of maniacal voices claiming control of their turf in the shadows of unconsciousness.

Dreams are just one more lens through which we can see our

lives and the world around us. Not the only or primary lens, but crucial I think, for a potent spiritual life. Thank you, Karl, for giving me back my dreams.

MASSACRE AT DAWN

Flat on my back
in bed
fingers plugging
both ears
eyes closed
holding in a dark placid lake
at the quiet of dawn.
The day is rising.
Spreading sunlight
washes over the beach of snow outside the window
and I can feel the motion of minions
inside my chest—or are they crawling up
the inside of my stomach?
Eight hours of dreamless sleep
should not end like this—
squirrels inside
rippling the calm
with their chattering, dithering
mania.

"Hold the stillness!" I urge,
my own voice echoing inside.

Slowly, rhythmically, I inhale
and then allow the warmed air
to slowly wash out.
Breathe in,
breathe out—
slowing the river of life,
feeling it flowing all the way down
filling my belly—
darkness behind my shuttered eyes
now holding the center steady
with calm.

Oh no, they are coming.

"REM"

—is said to keep us well

Rapid Eye Movement
is a place to luxuriate
each evening,
and alone,
to keep from going crazy,
getting sick.

REM
sounds more graceful,
less mechanical.
A spa or dark nest
of consciousness – a realm
where doughy fat children
hang-time with Michael and LeBron,
old men receive salacious visits
from soft-skinned women, and
young women meet men who thrill them
in body, mind, and spirit.
Or perhaps,

my dreams are too dog-eared
and traditional,
because some men dream about men
and some women, women,
and any
of the above and
lots more.

I've lost the address though.

Last night I never arrived.
The harder I tried to find REM
the more frantic
the darkness swirled within me.

I did dream
at least one dream.
Old college classmates
had grown into right-wing militants
acting like bow-tied chums
and worshiping drunken caterwauling humor—
the kind that jams a seed in my teeth.
Then, suddenly,
I was climbing a steep embankment

alongside dozens of old men
each of them, but not me, knew the way—
and what we were running from.
Wheezing
knees burning
pulling myself up the incline
clutching deeply rooted tufts of grass—
somehow, I knew my car was up there,
my only means of escape
still eclipsed by the ridge above.

But the dream did not feel
like Rapid Eye Movement.
I woke as if I had never slept.
My eyelids thick
and burning, fog
a heavy dew on my brain.
Adrift in exile
too awake to sleep,
too tired
to feel rested,
I must make amends
with the day
in slow motion.

Too many nights like this
and crazy won't begin to name it.

THE WOUNDED ANIMAL SPEAKS

My chest heaves
with swelling until it hurts,
the red meat of muscle
pushed outward
to the ends of its sinuous rope.

Then, violently,
the plunger of collapsing lungs
sucks the chest cavity dry,
every molecule of oxygen exhausted out.
A new river of air surges
an unrelenting torrent
flooding the cavern
burning the throat—
lungs afire
muscles enflamed.

Running, running,
running
without ever moving.

My heart blisters
from swallowed blood
bubbling through arteries
engorged by too much running.
Chased by no one,
fleeing in fear,
the hot breath of something
moist upon my neck.
I have been running
forever.

Today, it stops. Now.

The wounded animal
emits a crackling
high whine, then harbors
a low
barely audible
growl.

It squats
in the dark shadows of my brain.
Its haunches rounded down,
tail curled underneath wet legs, fur frayed,

greasy, and streaked.
An exposed wound
pinned like a rose on a caved-in shoulder
shines, the skin peeled in slices
opening a bloom of glistening red
with a fat worm of organ hanging from it.
Those yellow eyes glow
in that darkened corner
under crazed light
flashing panic
or assault.

No more running from it.
Today, live or die,
I stop.

The wounded animal inside
and me
will meet.

AT THE BOTTOM OF MY HEART

Rifling the heart
with bloody folds
and ragged with scar-tissue,
the walls are dimpled from incoming
and form deep trenches of muscle.
Whatever sinks
into these lightless canyons
is irretrievably lost—
except from dreams
or memories of trauma.

Ghosts and ghouls
and dark fairies
of an unnamed kind
glide on currents
hovering over the carrion
of decomposing shame.
Ignominy
regret
repulsion

remorse

a sticky silt covers

slick rubbery sinew.

These ravines,

deep below navigable blue veins,

are troughs collecting detritus

from ignoble deeds

and worse thoughts.

Gravity cannot pull forgiveness so deep

and light will not penetrate.

Up on the sunny surface

promises of magical forgiveness

echo between glistening waves

releasing thin joyous breezes.

But below,

a single

lonely diving bell

hazards recovery.

I am the only pilot

able to reach such deep channels of shame—

and you

the only one in yours.

Jung said, we do not "become enlightened
by imagining figures of light,
but by making the darkness conscious."

Rig for depth.
Clear the bridge.
Dive, dive, dive.

ALONE

In the darkness
only four eyes see—
    mine,
and two more looking out
from the closest fear.

Short Story: "The Desolation"

—A Jesus Tale based on Mark 1:9-13

Dark silhouettes standing against a waning sunset, arms stretch upward to heaven in prayer, hands open with fingers grasping for God, and the stillness of desert wind syncopated by sassy larks and peepers—that is how I remember us most often. Nearly every evening, at home or on the road, or even in the large meetings we held among the villages, when the sky was touched with pinks and oranges and darkening grays, we all fell into stillness. That was his rule, or should I say his gift to us: silence at sunset. As if by prearrangement with the sun and moon and nesting birds, all words ceased. When it stormed or clouds hung low and thick, masking the occasion, we somehow still knew when to begin. And then without a signal, we picked back up again, sometimes resuming the conversation precisely where we left off.

I have always thought his allegiance to silence was a residue of his wilderness time. When he left John that day at the river, he told us of the strange and frightening travail that followed. He began walking after the baptism. He was in a stupor so that hours or maybe even days went by without his remembering. He found himself in the wilderness east of the Jordan. In our tongue it is called, *Yesh i Mon*. Goi'im call it *The Desolation*.

It is a desolation. Yesh i Mon is four days long and two days across. On the west, it ends where the land has been broken away and falls into the salty lake. It stops at the great white cliffs no one can climb. On the other side of Yesh i Mon, the wilderness gives way to life: flat green pastures cradle sheep and village roads crisscross like the veins on the back of your hand. At the northern tip of Yesh i Mon, the Jordan River is strong and feeds the earth. At the southern end, the earth is withered and cracked because there is no river.

Yesh i Mon is woven with naked hills the wind and rain have carved into strange statues from the rock. There is no soil in Yesh i Mon, only dust. Puddles of grass and tiny wildflowers spot secluded troughs in the rock where all the soil has collected. Life clutches wherever it can in Yesh i Mon. There are no trees, but huge boulders cast dark shadows and they almost seem to breathe in the sweltering temperatures as clear, ghostly waves of heat rise from their sizzling surface.

The only rain comes all at once and ruts the chalky rock with furrows and folds like the wrinkles on an old peasant's face. Just as suddenly, the rain disappears into the thirsty stone. This land, this desolation, is the home of spirits. Those who live at her edge will tell you stories about the war that rages in the dark of Yesh i Mon. It is a war between the powers of light and the powers of darkness. Fierce sounds of battle can often be heard echoing within the desolation. It has long been said that The One who is to come and return The Land to us, will emerge from Yesh i Mon victorious over the powers of darkness.

Jesus did not know how long he was out there in Yesh i Mon, a month or maybe longer. There was little for him to eat in the wilderness, and he got so hungry that he took to eating lizards and bugs. Crunching those horrid hard shelled little bugs and chewing a lizard when it was still warm were tastes he could never spit out of his mouth, even years later. At first, he wretched, but as the days went by and he climbed over rocks and ravines in the sun, the shriveling of his stomach numbed him. At times Jesus was delirious and his lips bubbled and popped from the dry heat. He had no sense of where he was and with each step the madness gripped him. The sun, the thirst, the hunger, and the echoing aloneness crippled his senses. He was lost. His visions and nightmares confirmed it.

He leaped forward from a dead sleep one day, when the shadow of a figure pierced through him like an icy wind. It was a man. He was clean, well dressed, well fed. The man held out a water skin and Jesus drank until he was bloated, but he still gorged the bread that followed. It was offered to him without a word from the man. As Jesus ate and drank like a dog, he kept his eyes on the stranger. The man seemed familiar, but he never spoke.

They kept an uneasy company for several days, the man who

would not speak and Jesus. Jesus could find out nothing of who he was, why he had stopped, or what he wanted. Like a starving mongrel he was fed scraps at the door, so Jesus followed his master who seemed to know which way to walk.

In the daytime, as they walked, Jesus followed and tried to coax the man to speak. At night he was afraid to sleep, mistrusting the stranger who slumbered easily across the campfire from him. In the pit of his stomach, Jesus knew this man was sinister. He knew that he was being led by his deprivation and he remembered the snake he once watched lay motionless in the sand until a rat came along. Jesus knew he was the rat, but he didn't know what kind of snake the voiceless shadow would turn out to be. Jesus wanted to run and hide, sometimes to attack and kill. But he needed a way out of the desolation more than he needed an end to his fear.

Then one night, Jesus woke with a start to the sound of firewood crackling and popping. The stranger was gone. On top the ash blanketed coals lay a smoldering, blackened scroll of Torah. Jesus ran out into the darkness of the desert and screamed for the man: "Who are you? Who are you!" Then Jesus woke up in truth. There was no man, fire, or Torah.

It was daybreak and he found himself back at the river near where John baptized him. The stranger had been the last of his night visions while he was lost in Yesh i Mon. "But he is real,"

Jesus would tell us often. "He is real, and he lives within me. He lives in the shadows I would ignore, and he is there in the darkness within you." Then Jesus would warn us to know our darkness and not pretend it wasn't there. I'm not sure I have ever understood, but in those sunsets fading into darkness, in the stillness and silence, I always remembered that at the edge of our peaceful calm was another kind of silence where a stranger lurked among friends.

"Yesh i Mon is in you, don't get lost," Jesus would sometimes whisper.

Living

Essay: "A 'Good' Life"

The day we buried my father the church was full. But this is about life not death.

He was introverted, painfully so. He lived in the town where he was born, and the city knew him from longevity not celebrity. I would credit it to the shear accumulation of small unremarkable acts of decency—which was the substance of his life.

My dad played basketball in the days before the dribble, when the game was about passing with very little motion. A classmate of his, a beat cop who seemed to me the size of Shaquille O'Neal when I was a boy, told me once that my dad played as slowly as he lived.

He made things with his hands—the deliberate patience of his soul guiding hammer, saw, router, or grinder toward smooth and shapely conclusions. Shelf or boat, he birthed them slowly from nothing into something smooth, clean, true.

I never knew him to play. There was no hop or trick in him. When he played cards, he was a silent partner. Humor operated with only two gears: a slight but charming grin, and on occasion, a silent shuddering laughter that brought tears to his eyes. I loved the latter because it wrapped everyone else in warmth and joy.

He was meticulous. When painting, cutting the grass, or even building a fiberglass kayak in the basement, whatever he used never made it onto his clothing or the floor. When working for fun, but always for function, he wore the pants of a worn-out suit and an old white dress shirt, miraculously missing wrinkles, smudges, and stains.

A solo attorney, he quietly gave himself to his hometown. Offering legal aid before there was such a thing was the libertarian extension of his compassion and care, in hopes of keeping the government out of it. If you asked him why he helped so many he would demur, preferring to live silently without declaration.

I grew up a sapling in his shade, "Little Bob" to his friends who would smile, pat me on the head, and inevitably say something affirming about my father. Others, too, knew me as his—those who visited our neighborhood only to be hired to clean houses and mow lawns. What reason did they have to reverence him? I would come to find out.

I was extroverted, showy, and venturesome right from the start—traits that did not weep from his genes into mine. I traveled into homes and places he never did. On the county hiway crew—summer college money for me and year-round livelihood for those working around me—fighting was recreational. The big college kid was a target. A grizzled, toothless Appalachian man I had already had to fight totally changed his attitude toward me when he found out Bob Miller was my dad.

"That man your pa?" he asked. His voice and face turned soft. "He wast the onlyest to take my divorce. Paid what I could and that was okay wit him." After he discovered I was Bob Miller's son, he left me alone that summer and the next.

Those summers, and other times too, when I drifted over the color line that ran through that town like white down the spine of a skunk, they knew him. Turtle shy, slow and wordless to a fault, somehow my dad was known across the invisible hard boundaries of race and class in that average American city.

He walked to work or took the bus and spent whatever money he made on a wife and kids, as extravagant as he was simple. He ended up with little left over for himself. He worked until he was eighty and his legs felt heavy and painful. His hearing struggled to decipher more than low grade thuds. Begrudgingly, he first let go of lawyering and eventually his volunteering for Audubon, Church, Library, and the Historical Society.

He ate with the same moderation he lived, except for cookies.

He smoked with moderation, until he quit at seventy when his wife was stricken with COPD. He drank port with moderation and liked a dry martini with a green olive.

He was not the best at anything. No single thing he did turned the course of history. Nobody gives awards for integrity—that hard to measure distance between what we say we value and how we actually live. So, he was never lauded for his tiptoed acts of kindness and discreet public service because in truth, his own left hand may not have known what his right had done.

As slowly as he played basketball and lived his life, his ninety-three years melted away. Just a day after his dog gave up the ghost, my dad took his last breath. We buried their ashes together.

Most of the people who filled the church that day came with remembrances told to them by an uncle, a mom, dad, or friend. A few, who were half a generation younger than him, and among the cohort who had met downtown for coffee and lunch each workday for decades, came to say goodbye. But mostly he was remembered that day by younger people. They may not even have remembered him themselves but remembered those who knew him. They marveled at a life of quiet honor, steady fairness, just plain kindness, and other quiet virtues—gentleness, humility, compassion.

What is a good life? It may be one like his, unmeasured because unadorned.

What seems true to me, is that people from all walks of life, who saw the world in different colors and shapes from one another, saw him as good. As a "good man." I can think of no greater epitaph than the one I so often heard attributed to my father, a good man (person).

BROWN LEAF

An unsettling early morning walk— – no, more than unsettling—it
rattled my bones.
Bones know.

It was the same walk
walked each day,
dog in lead
or pulled by me.

Out the long drive

turn right

right again at the corner

then left

between two grandmother beech

cross the street

left again

back to the corner
another left
toward the driveway
and one final

left.

A routine— - even drudgery most days.
But this day a wordless caution rises in me
    at the patina of ice,
a sheet of frozen mist
neatly spread
by a warmer night
turning colder
at the morning's edge.

But the breath of snow hiding the ice
incites puppiness
and prancing
from she who must be loved.

My knees chatter fretfully,
ruminating about pain,
balance,
shots,
surgery.

Dog—carefree, prancing, primed

to romp.

Me—
a fussing nebbish
so completely distracted I almost missed
the fingertip catch,
a small clarion
noticed
from the corner of my eye
but nearly missed.

One brown curled fist of a leaf
    hanging by a frail stem
    twisting
    and reeling in the wind.

Mid-December is early
for an oak to give up her leaves,
yet there she was, bare
but for one child left hanging.

I do not want to be that leaf.

Dog burbling from even a thin dusting of snow,
        she is so pleased to be alive in the cold.
Undaunted by hunger, indifferent
to bowel or bladder,
arrested by pure joy—
utterly alive,
spiritually unconstrained,
even by her blue collar and leash.

I was a curled,
dry leaf   hanging on

worrying about ice.

Some days,
hanging on is what we do.
Not even against all odds,

but modus operandi.

    Sure. There is suffering.

Pain. Grief.

Sorrow and woe—

lake of lava beneath

the plank we teeter down.

        Dog doesn't think about it.

She does not inhale the inevitability and

exhale the angst. She joys.

The only way joy is joy.

So, stop it, already,

I told myself.

COME OF AGE

Tiptoe
into the soft
tissue of your brain.
Bend over in the darkness,
lift the flap on a memory. See it?

Those are your
supple, never calloused
feet slipping into your mommy's
high heels or daddy's wingtips.

Fast forward:
Hear yourself chuckle
at the wobbling determination
of your own child, niece, or nephew
shuffling across the living room,
teeny tiny feet swimming inside your Crocs or Keens.

In real time now,
your grandchild runs free

in an adult tee—a shirt too snug for you,
But a floor-length nightgown for him, her, them.

Oh, the exquisite
shelter of a body so much
bigger than our own. Oh, the goodness
of our tiny fingers enfolded in the cocoon of
a warm strong hand so much larger than our own.

Grown up now,
or even old, we are hunkered
down underneath a domed sky. The
crushing weight of gravity holds us low
on this fragile planet, hanging small and defenseless
in a distant corner of the darkness, surrounded by far distant lights.

Now, daytime sobriety
presses in with nighttime vengeance,
keeping us slogging, one foot
at a time through the muddy ordinary.

Now, we
feel the fingerless

stumps of our threadbare
nature, thin and vulnerable as it is
swallowed by an enormous, indifferent Cosmos.

Oh but for a roomy shoe
or larger warm hand
curled 'round
our own.

CHANGE

I just want to try it over there,
putting the chair in the corner where
it won't stick out so much— - or wait!
There, with the end table
between it and the sofa. No.
I liked it better
where it was
before.

Change can be
a thirst,
a swollen throat,
a scratching for moisture
to relieve the soreness - a palliative.
When the furniture is moved,
I can see the cracks in the walls.
I can see the room anew.
That cataract of complacency dissolves—
washed by the rain of change.

But when change reigns,
thirst becomes fear—
tremulous motions deep in the bowels,
quivering the belly,
ratcheting tightness around the heart.
It is one thing to move the furniture,
but a bowling ball straight down the alley
knocks real lives akimbo, sprawling chaos.
It can be horror.

Change begins with a granular pebble
living atop a pile of stones,
high above the tree line of human perspective.
It rests there,
impervious to wind
or rain or drought
or feeble human efforts to construct a world. Then,
most often for reasons far beyond
our database and theories— -
perhaps even for reasons that transpire
among the stars - a pebble rolls.
Even if we see it happen,
we likely keep walking,
blind to the mountain

of rock

soon to bury us.

Essay: "Slap me!"

Try this out and you'll be amazed.

Face someone while standing up (this should be a friend who trusts you, and who you trust), and pretend to slap him or her with your right hand. Now, have them turn the other cheek for you to slap it. In order to slap that second cheek with your right hand, you will have to do it backhanded—as in, slap them with the back of your hand.

Why is this important? Because "turning the other cheek" was an act of non-violent resistance rather than passive despondency or forced humility.

What we need to know about this familiar but often misused proverbial teaching, is that slapping someone with the open hand (or palm side) was an act of social dominance in the first century, from whence the proverbial saying comes. It was something that a person of social stature would do to one of lesser stature—a soldier for instance, to a peasant. But a backhanded slap was reserved for a social equal.

By turning the other cheek, literally, a peasant was taunting the aggressor to slap him or her as an equal.

I first learned this tidbit from Walter Wink, a twentieth century biblical scholar and theologian. With this, and many other such subversive teachings, a first century rabbi named Jesus armed ordinary peasants who didn't stand a chance of succeeding with violence, to trick their oppressors into acknowledging their dignity.

I have discovered that the writings of sages and mystics—from Judaism, Islam, Christianity, and Buddhism—often lose their radical flavor when presented through the sieve of institutional religion. Organized religion tends to domesticate its gods, to make them more manageable, and to avoid any risks to their institutional interests.

That is not very different from governments either.

How often is the truly radical nature of the Bill of Rights taught in our schools? How often is the extreme inhumanity of our national heroes revealed when it comes to their behavior and attitudes around slavery or the genocide of Native Americans? The history of our war crimes is essentially left off the table in school as well. We domesticate our civics lessons to bolster nationalism, and to keep it from getting in the way of unadulterated patriotism.

In fact, the modern discipline of history truly began as a means of promoting nationalistic propaganda and, much to the chagrin of governments, unintentionally evolved into an academic study. It now seems to be devolving back to its roots, aided by a hard push from state governments and school boards as they edit textbooks to jibe with white nationalist mythology.

We would do better to sidle up to the texts of history, whether secular or religious, with an open mind, instead of seeking to reinforce our preset ideas. If we can put down our agendas and come to the historical texts with truly open eyes, ears, and hearts, they will offer us amazing insights and surprises. In fact, it will likely change our hearts and minds.

Come to think of it, that is probably why we seldom do.

Healing

Confession: "Virginia"

A mother is someone upon whom we superimpose our projections. Those projections are partly composed of images cast by the light within our own eyes, and partially from those swirling particles engulfed in our shadows inside. No one knows their mother, not truly.

My mother suffered from undiagnosed mental illness, that's my best guess. Depression, surely, substance abuse maybe, and some pernicious kind of anxiety. But like I said, no one knows his or her mother truly, so try not to misjudge mine from these projections.

I knew her away from the theater of Thanksgiving and Christmas, which she produced with great fanfare each year for the returning heroes of her motherhood. As the youngest of five and last one home, I witnessed her leaning on her elbows in silence at the yellow linoleum kitchen table, staring into nothing at one in the morning. She sat there unresponsive to any query or cajoling I might cast her way. With the older children dismissed to their lives in what seemed lands far away, I witnessed my mother fighting the hard demons that howl at all of us as we traverse our fifties. She seemed all alone, shut up inside and only coming out for air when she had to. A more mature, compassionate son would have done what he could to help her, but I was caught up in my own struggles that insured her even greater torment.

I knew my mother as the one she failed with, who rarely, if ever, met her expectations, and was the subject of her derision. When stern orders did not work, humiliation was her cat o' nine tails. She likely learned the ways of humiliation at the hands of her mother because she wielded it lithely and with confidence. Oddly, I do not remember her employing the whip of humiliation on my older siblings, but that may only be the complete self-centeredness of a child's memory, and of the youngest child at that.

For the first dozen years, as best I can remember, fear and want bifurcated my tender psyche. Fear of my mother's shaming criticism and deep yearning for her love to be expressed with affirmation. The next two dozen years were a stew of angry resentments, a confused one-foot-in and one-foot-out relationship, with deep dives into therapy. The next twenty years with children of my own refined the sieve of memory and provided a more generous and compassionate perspective. Therapy in my fifties, especially Jungian therapy, created a whole new playing field for exercising the memories of my past.

There was a big "Ah Ha!" moment about my mom that came embarrassingly late, I admit. Sometime around sixty I realized that when I graduated from high school, my mother was not allowed to have her own credit card. It wasn't until I was in college, in 1974 to be exact, that Congress passed legislation allowing women to establish their own credit. Everything about my mother's life and choices that was limited simply because she was a woman would have felt infantilizing to her—which of course, it was.

But Virginia was brilliant. She went to college at age sixteen after skipping multiple grades. But when her father died suddenly, so did her options. She had to quit the University of Michigan and do one of the few things women were allowed to do, become a secretary. She went to New York City, to Katherine Gibbs Secretarial School—something we did not know until late in her life. To this day I do not know what her short work history included, but when she married my dad and began having children, she never worked outside the home again.

She could have. As we grew up, she could have enrolled in the state university across the street from where we lived, but she thought that particular college was beneath her. She knew her own brilliance.

Somehow, in her own mind, she had also elevated herself to Brahmin social status without the credentials to grant it. Social anxiety mixed with a secret shame over being adopted, along with bottled up genius and potential that never found expression, led my mother into a hole from which she never fully emerged. I regret the decades I spent blaming her for all the ways I felt she victimized me without ever considering the personal and social wounds she carried.

She had contemporaries who made other choices, doggedly fought back and made their way past the limits patriarchy and misogyny forced upon them. She could have done that too, but for reasons I will never be able to fully understand or appreciate, she did not. There are places I have never gone that I could have, and ceilings I lowered rather than raised for reasons both known and hidden— and I am a white, heterosexual male from an upper middle-class family. I do not know the demons my mother wrestled with, but from the outside looking in, it seems like she lost many of the battles.

The last time I saw my mother alive we made peace, the best we could. She was eighty-three and I was forty-six. She was wildly anxious about death, to the point that she would not allow us to leave her alone at night. In a hospital bed at home, coming to the end of a ten-year downward stair-step descent into the unknown abyss, my mother required someone to be next to her bed, holding her hand, all night long. If she awoke in the night and no one was there, she would yell for help. Though her lungs were riddled from fifty years of copious cigarettes and COPD, she could still open her throat and sound an alarm that would echo throughout the house.

I lived three and a half hours away and did not travel back as often as I should have to help my sister who opted to live with our parents until their deaths. With four children under twelve at home and a demanding job, I felt that stabbing guilt and frustration known to those who watch from afar as others steward a parent toward the end of life.

On watch during the night the last time I saw her alive, I slept fitfully in the Mission style chair pulled close to her bed. My arm threaded the chrome bars to hold her tiny, cold hand. I would awake at intervals with my arm completely numb to my shoulder. It felt as though the cold from her body crawled up through my fingers and was spreading toward my heart, consuming any warmth in its path. Startled, I would let go and shake life back into my arm, assure her with a gentle pat that I was still there, and await the next time she called for my hand to hold hers.

On that last night, sometime between two and four in the morning, I gurgled up the nerve to say it. "Mom, I am sorry for all the struggles we had, and for any hurt I caused you."

Why was that so hard to say? What depth of ego can resist such a small vulnerability? Or was it a depth of fragility that feared even a shallow exposure?

Simple fear was not why it was hard to say. The memory of painful experiences does not disappear with understanding. But still, I was a middle-aged man with children, and a professional caregiver who was good at coaching others through their struggles. My lowly attempt at reconciliation did not seem commensurate with the ground-swelling trepidation that caught in my throat for several attempts before it finally came out.

Then, perhaps the fear was justified. My words were met with silence. Nothing returned from the darkness surrounding the body in the bed at the other end of my arm.

All those years of pain, struggle, confusion, resistance, aggression, desire, and hope traveled through that darkness. Up and down the fire escape of therapy and understanding that ran alongside all those memories, was the simple desire for her voice to emerge from the darkness. When nothing came forward, I labored through the work of understanding to melt my raw emotions into the steel of reason. I was still working at it when a small voice arrived.

"We did the best we could."

She said nothing else. It was enough. I smiled and repeated it back to her: "Yes, we did the best we could."

CONFUSED BY THE PRESENCE OF ABSENCE AND THE EMPTINESS OF HOPE

It started in a dream
then leaked into my pillow.

In the dark shroud of sleep,
an arc of sparking synapse flashed brightly,
exposing a writhing entanglement
of arms, roving hands,
and pulsating hidden capillaries.
The entire planet of my body
radiated outwardly
a brilliant energy
leaving the shield of my chest
and fusing with the near presence of unknown breasts.
This is the moment of explosion;
the Big Bang of electric emotions.

But no!
At the very moment of ignition
everything disappeared.

Dream ended. Down
a gaping hole of grief
the passion plunged,
swirling through a dark drain of emptiness.

Is absence a feeling?

When a hole is filled
absence leaves.
But where does it go?
Can it reside,
still hidden,
within a space now crammed
and obliterated
by presence?

Is this sobbing
and choking
on loss,
about something
or nothing?

That wail—
the one just escaping my lips

and now echoing back at me
across the dark chamber of sleep?
As it lands on my pillow
consummated by actual tears, no longer dreaming,
is it bemoaning the absence of something
or the presence of it?

The dream was real, really
filling the moment
before it was gone.

Suddenly awake
in thin morning light, I panic
not knowing if these tears
are about something or nothing?
These salty warm beads
rolling down the hill of my cheek
to the swell of lips
are they about someone
or the absence of someone?

Absence is a something.
Sucking away everything
from all other somethings,

it is something too.
Absence is not a nothing.
But what then is hope—
an empty bucket?

How is it that absence—
                    a nothing after all—

swallows up everything?
Yet, hope—
an empty something—
is composed of so little,
yet fills so much?

MULTIVERSE

Before the sun burned off the pillow of fog,
half of Long Pier still hidden under it,
the restaurant voices of unseen geese
honked incessantly
in the miasma above.
Astonishment prickled my skin
as slices of blue,
higher up,
above the fog,
above the clouds,
opened small portholes to the far beyond.
Perhaps we live in a multiverse after all? The thought
reaching up into those holes.

The thought caught in my brain—
which is a Dali-verse, whispering
absurdities during the day
and dreams strafing it at night.
With a vengeance,
loud voices
and intruding images

arrive—that woman
with the wrong man, the one I don't know well
who nonetheless floats in my dream
as if a clock folding over an armchair
in the actual Dali-verse.
Or the illness I haven't contracted, yet.
Even a puddle
of flammable anxiety
still leaking from a remembered childhood event.
These somethings throb beneath the dank soil
of memory,
twitching and alive.
What they are is still not told.

I am in another place,
at another time,
concurrent
with the woman and man in my dreams, before the illness
that hasn't happened yet,
and before my memory.
Asleep or awake
too many parallels to track.

These invisible encounters breathe
beneath any moment,

inside the blossom of other memories
forgotten not gone.
Ego-logical time
layered in dreams,
rings of embedded experience,
forming striations in the brain -
a multiverse of memories
    inside the cosmos within.

Let me stay focused:
on the lake,
the pier,
the unseen geese overhead,
the blue sky high above the blanket of grey.
Stand still in this verse,
leave the multiverse alone.

FOR DECLAN AND WESLEY

There are monsters under the bed
in my head,
in my head.
Monsters under my bed!

I'll get my dog and a flashlight too,
and mom's pointy shoe,
and mom's pointy shoe.
Show that monster a thing or two!

Lifted the bedspread and to my surprise
There weren't no monsters
and no scary eyes,
no scary eyes.
Going to sleep now,

with dog and panda close by.

BEFORE I CIRCLE THE DRAIN

On my way to circling the drain
in the last year or month or day,
I want to open my arms
and fall away
with utter thanksgiving.

Whether free fall
or tight wiggle through a tunnel to light,
I want to consummate my small life
with a final gush of gratitude.

There is work to do.

Death could come by a thousand cuts
from injury or disease,
and harder still
to be ready in an instant
for an unexpected guillotine.
Even if it is a long slow walk,
under the shadow of outliving friends,

when the ringing of loneliness
echoes through the universe,
I hope to lace melancholy with thanksgiving.

I best get ready now.

"Thank you, God,"
or whatever
delivered to me
this spectacular serendipity
someone else might call
humdrum.
Outside looking in
they may question its value.
But as for me, "Thank you."

TORCHLIGHT TOURS OF THE PSYCHE

No cameras or recordings, please.
All bags checked at the entrance.
Torchlight tours are to be taken at your own risk.

Limited itinerary:
three caverns—dark chambers,
one entry,
one exit,
no other outlets.

The first cavern, my chest cavity,
is generous --
spacious even,
a deep placid lake
easily navigated by dugout.
Torchlight is reflected on calm rippling waters.
A yellow three-sided CAUTION sign appears:
"Rumbles and quakes elsewhere
swell turbulence here,
reverberations of sound
force crushing air pressure

as heartbreak and grief
curdle the blood,
lesions on the walls will scream."

Next, we enter the Sacral Chakra --
septic tank
or gutter bowels.
By whatever name,
this is a river Styx
crossing over to gods of the underworld.
It's a happy, well-fed place
until it isn't.
Then all Hell breaks loose.
Alluvial plains of hardened cesspools
rise up in tidal waves,
swallowing any poor bastard navigating the surface
down a puckered hole.

The final frontier of this journey
is a cavern of delirium
where legions of thoughts
whisper ceaselessly.
Frenzied wisps of phantasm
thrash goblins of memory.

There is blood in the water for sharks of the mind.
Tours can begin or end here,
but they risk becoming lost
when turning into this looping cranial maze
with no exit.

Torchlight tours
paddling these interior caverns
are now closed
to the General Public.
Solo voyages only, for the foolhardy proprietor
or an Urgent Care specialist.

Spirituality

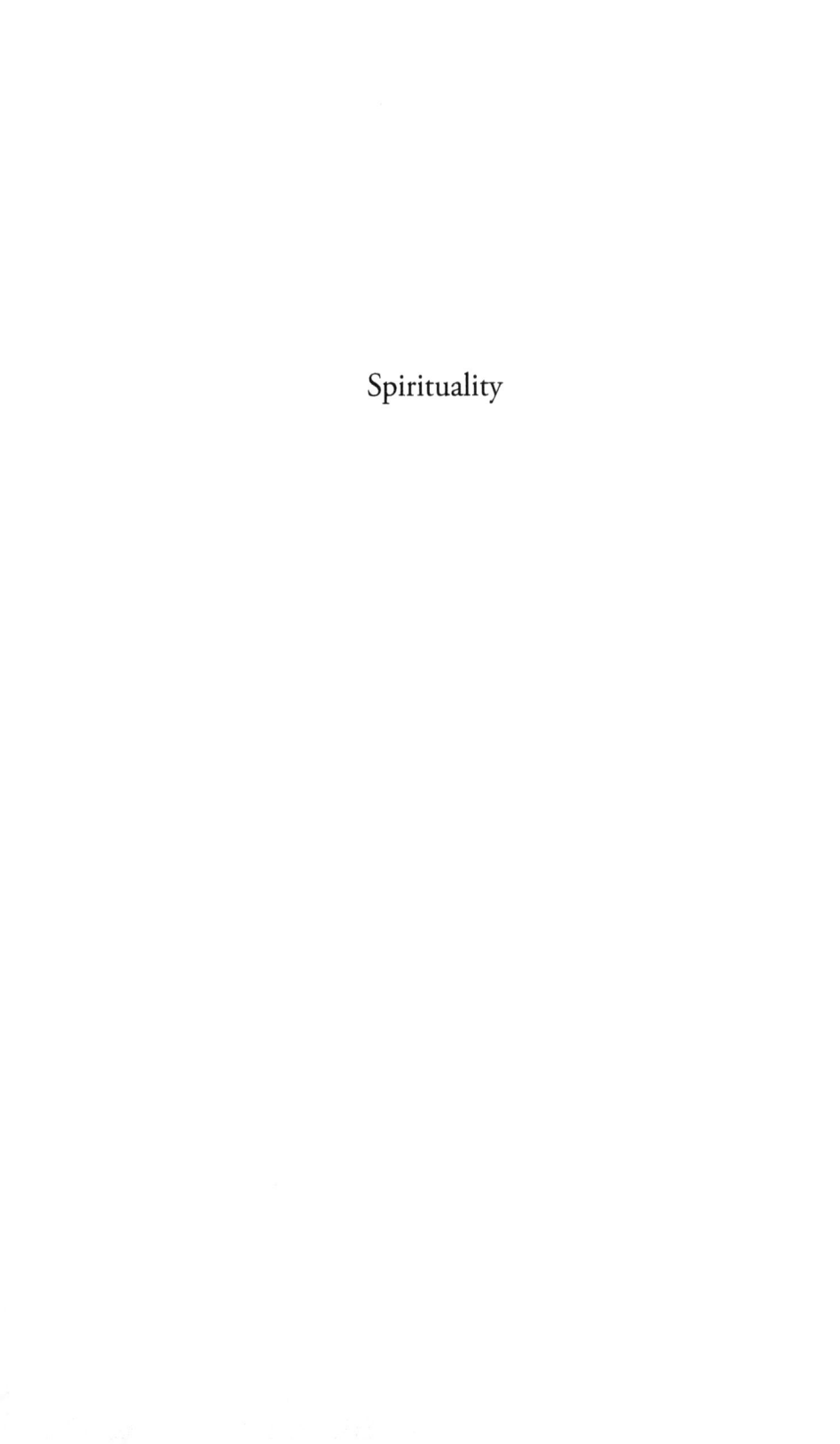

Essay: "A Christian Manifesto"

"You didn't die for my sins," I say across the counter into the kitchen where no one is standing, "I know you didn't." Then, just to be safe, "Did you?"

The grain of ambivalence is a stone in my shoe, a knowing that I know nothing. It is a vulnerability. Knowing that nothing about what I most want to know is ever truly known, keeps me humble and sometimes stung into inaction. I mean really, who is going to go down for the count or be burned at the stake for something they can't be sure of? Occasionally, eventually, deadly decisions may have to be made. It would be much easier to make them with an army of certainty behind us.

But truly, Jesus did not die on the cross for our sins. That is so absurd it hardly bears argument. While God is not bound by human reason, neither is there any evidence that God operates with insane incoherence, and that is what the idea of Jesus dying for everyone's sins is, incoherent. It makes no reasonable sense, not even a little.

Meanwhile, there is an utterly sensible reason for Jesus to die on the cross. Not for our sins, but because of our sins.

Jesus died because people with power do not give it away.

From the lowest street urchin who is the alpha of his or her pack, to the CEO, Prime Minister, or President—when we have power, we use it to manage and get more power. We do not give it away for free. So, Jesus died at the hands of those with coercive power who had no intention of sharing it. Why? Because God is all about greater distribution of power.

Jesus was convicted of insurrection against the power of Rome, Pontus Pilate nailed the indictment on the cross above his head. The usual punishment for such foolhardiness was crucifixion. It is right there in the text if we take the words seriously. He was hailed king when there was already a king in place. Goodbye Jesus.

The early Gospel editors, gentiles writing for a Roman world, had to explain away that stone-hard artifact of history. But the explanations they came up with were as goofy as this later idea: God set up Jesus to be tortured and suffer a horrendous death so people thousands of years later could be forgiven.

What interests me is the resistance Christians—and other religions for that matter—have against changing our understanding of the meaning of seminal events. Historical events take place, but the meaning of those events can and does change as historical perspective provides new angles and lenses through which to see them. Just because the original advocates, adherents, and hearers believed something, doesn't make it a good belief for us.

There is a Wikipedia-size file of events, ideas, discoveries, and changes that have taken place within human culture since the time of Jesus. So, what makes the perspective of an anonymous first century gospel editor, the absolute right one? Even a known personality like Paul, who organized early Christian communities and wrote letters we still have today, was well-educated by first century standards, but spectacularly ignorant by ours. Why are we stuck with his ideas, especially when he didn't know Jesus either?

Most of us can acknowledge the fact that none of the gospels were assembled and circulated until one-and-a-half to two generations after Jesus was executed; in the case of John, it was three full generations later. The people who edited these free-standing and disconnected stories into books had a focused agenda. But what makes us think they had a better handle on Jesus and the events of Jesus' life and death, than we do?

It scares some people to ask these obvious questions because they do not want that stone in the shoe called uncertainty. As irksome and sometimes painful as it is to embrace the existential uncertainty of authentic faith, it is also liberating. We are now free to make sense out of the stories, rather than have them defy our reason and experience. These stories can be about God in the real world as we live it, rather than magical and wishful thinking. Isn't that worth more than the discomfort of uncertainty?

"Back to you Jesus," I say, now in the living room in my ergonomic recliner. Jesus doesn't answer, but he does not seem fragile and scared either.

I have no idea what Jesus' relationship to God was, any more than I could sum up my relationship with God in stark and material terms. We call Jesus "Christ," which is the Greek translation of the Hebrew concept of "Messiah." What Messiah literally meant was "oily head."

Messiah meant "anointed" and it indicated that God had chosen someone for a particular purpose, as in a king, queen, or prophet of Israel. There were even people outside Israel recognized as anointed by God for a specific purpose. Cyrus, King of Persia comes to mind.

An updated version of this idea happens at baptism, when we make the sign of the cross with holy oil on the newly baptized forehead. We say they are, "marked as Christ's own forever." So, it is not difficult to imagine Jesus was anointed as God's own and pointed toward a particular purpose that had to do with revealing something about the love of God. That is not an unreasonable idea, if we begin with the assumption God does in fact exist. But believing Jesus was God himself, that is a far greater reach.

Honestly, I don't want Jesus to be God.

What I know of God is that God is too much. It is actually more accurate to say I know about God, rather than I know God. The very nature of God is not to be known. What I do know about God is well represented by the climactic scene at the end of *Indiana Jones: Raiders of the Lost Ark*. The unsuspecting, lust-filled, and power-hungry Nazis open the Lost Ark that reportedly houses God. They want the power (remember, it is all about power with us). Out flies a beautiful wisp of light that suddenly becomes so intense it melts the flesh right off the bones of those standing in its presence. Then all the remaining bones and faces explode. That is God.

God is too powerful for us. God is too much of whatever God is for us to even stand in its presence. We cannot exist in God's presence because, well, because God is God, and we are puny. God is all that is, and we are but an infinitesimal smudge on a teeny tiny planet unremarkable among the cosmos of drifting, spinning orbs. A part cannot know the whole. We gaze upon those amazing photographs from the James Webb telescope and exclaim how beautiful star formation, for example, is. Yet, we would disappear in a little blue flame were we to get within a million light years of it. God is the creator of everything, we are not even a crumb. How then, do we imagine we can know God?

Never mind the absolute non-sensible notion that Jesus is somehow God. If Jesus were God instead of human, then he does not mean much to us. We are not God. What we need are more and better human role models. Jesus gives us a better incarnation of humanness.

You probably will not believe this, but parables, proverbs, and proverbial sayings attributed to Jesus are astounding. They are not all equal to be sure, but the core wisdom associated with Jesus can evoke awed speechlessness, just as the Harvest Moon suspended low over the corn can lock the tongue and mist the eyes.

The uncertainty inherent in a completely human messiah and prophet is more than made up for in the wisdom revealed by coming to terms with that man's marvelous teachings. If we take our focus off the torture, execution, and empty tomb, then we will see more clearly the spiritual practice he offered. If only we had communities of people dedicated to his spiritual practice instead of to beliefs about him. I must imagine the world of human beings would be a different kind of place.

The world being a different kind of place is exactly what Jesus was and is about. Jesus asked, pleaded, prayed, and insisted that "thy kingdom come, on Earth as it is in heaven." That is his mission statement: The kingdom of heaven created here on earth. God will help with that, but it is essentially our work.

So, if you ask me what a Christian is—what Church is for—it is someone whose spiritual practice is aimed at bringing forth the kingdom of God on earth as it is in heaven. I don't care whether he or she believes in genies and leprechauns so long as they have a spiritual practice aimed at creatingt an earth that more nearly reflects our vision of heaven. Beliefs are a dime a dozen; practice is what matters.

THE LORD OF GENOCIDE

—What's Wrong with Matthew 21:33-46

He will put those wretches to a miserable death
in Auschwitz, Buchenwald, and Treblinka.
Then he will lease the vineyard to others
who will give him the produce at harvest—
no more stinginess and hoarding.

On with the Crusades,
then witch burnings
Southern lynchings
and Brokeback beatings.
We are the tenants now!

PARABLE

—Mathew 16:21-28

One man lashed himself to a tree.
Looping an anaconda-thick rope
around the oldest oak,
he pulled tight to gird his waist.
Looking down at the tree's gnarly feet
plunging into hardened soil,
he was pleased to imagine those spindly toes
gripping the earth, while above fat broad branches
hugged the sky.
It would give no ground in the coming storm.

Another man lingered unmoored.
He rocked back and forth on the porch
waiting for the tempest to arrive.
Waves came crawling up the planks,
fingers of death soon clawed his chair.
He rose calmly, like the eye
curled within the unfettered wind.
Perched for flight upon the railing of his porch,

he dove headfirst into the mouth of the storm,
disappearing between the white teeth of the ocean.

The tsunami unrolled an obliterating tongue,
licking away man and tree,
house and porch, tower and boat,
concrete and steel.

The man who trusted a tree to save his life
was never found.
The man who knew nothing would save him
washed ashore, battered and broken,
scarred and crippled—for
life.

PATHETIC LORD

—Mark 14:1-9

Her hands—
palms generously softened
for labors of touch—
lithe fingers gloved in warm oil,
soothing bony shoulders,
then slowly enfolding his nape.
They pause there before closing around the skull:
fingers then sliding smoothly behind the ears,
melting minuscule knots of angry muscle,
softening bitter tendons,
rolling the head as gently as an egg.

"Your hands, Harlot!
Smearing the Lord
with undulating evil."
His voice snarls,
but his hands dare not touch.

Next, someone else's hands, manly hands,

squeeze Jesus firmly on the shoulders.
Assuring words drip
from the half grin of this dark angel.
His fingers
crusty with blood,
reach into the breast pocket
of Jesus' new flannel coat.
He does it so easily to his prey—
stealing their identity,
money,
credit cards, house.
He's a scurrilous tax collector—
extorting, bribing, and embezzling holiness
from the Lord.

There were others, too—
pedophiles, pawnbrokers, pimps—
who all sit around the table,
yucking it up with Jesus.
Feasting.

Pathetic.

RESIST!

My faith is not an immigrant
carried in third-class,
nor a slave
shackled to planks
in the dark below.

Oh, that I could say
it bloomed in Iona, a thin
Celtic veil
flowing
between verdant green
and sapphire blue.
I would settle for Stonehenge, raised
with thick ankles and calves,
rudimentary grunts,
and primitive music.

But alas,

my people, their voices

in my blood whispering even now, drip
from the sharp blades
and tongues of iconoclasts.
Cromwell's soldiers landed in America!
The virus hidden among the masses
is now pitting the walls of cathedrals
and eroding small chapels.
The infectious agent
leaped
cell to cell, morphing
into soul-less capitalism, and then
again, to secularism,
the dead flotsam of the sacred
left in its wake.

This is where trust comes to die.
Here I mean, now I mean.

Here, amidst otherwise hopeful
immigrants who gather
around the table of their faith
and remember how it was
and who they are.

It takes time for this virus

to enter the bloodstream

and do its work—

to take away eyesight

and intuition,

our ability to see

and know

and feel

the ordinary, sacred things

here at our feet.

Without the land breathing through their bodies,

without the hands held around the table,

without the vision of life

greater than the sum of one,

faith dies.

So, resist.

Listen to a tree breathe.

Reach down and dirty your fingers in the soil.

Feel the ice on the lake.

Drive miles and miles just to see the stars.

Find other freaks like you,

who were infected but did not die.

Find a table,

with hands to hold around it.

Break bread, sip wine,

praise simplicity.

Look one another in the eyes

and feel the presence

of a power greater than yourselves.

Intuit.

Imagine.

Listen.

Hear more than your heartbeat.

Recover what your ancestors knew

and brought with them—their immigrant hearts.

Their faith.

MERCY

mercy appears:
a small distant spot
glowing red upon the mountain,
a bare trickle against dark stone and green foliage

mercy seems
quiet at first, a small dab upon the landscape,
undulating into serpentine trickles—
downhill wiggles

mercy unchecked
flows wider, wider and
hotter, hotter,
steamrolling anything and everything

mercy burns
fiercely, melting the heart,
withering the brain,
colossal collateral heat,

justice is
glacial, a rigid
brittle institutional anchor
no match for mercy—

when mercy
melts justice all hell breaks loose,
logic and order be damned
not to mention for-profit prisons.

PSALM 139

What if I could dance again?
What if, with
tendons pulled like taffy
and my fibrous heart softening—
these brittle toes uncurling—
I could dance again?

Your love is kneading these petrified muscles
toward doughy freshness.
You press upon me,
behind and before,
suckling notes
and fluid rhythm
up from suddenly nimble hips.

What if I could dance again?

Your presence is wafting
through innermost thoughts,
opening hidden doors

behind my eyes, wicking nectar
from wells that had run dry.

If I whisper back a wet kiss
from deep within darkened silence,
will the Fred of my broken days
twirl the Ginger
of my restless nights?

If you lay your hand upon me,
I will fathom prenatal dreams
and unfurl nascent hope,
and whisper unspoken passion
while writing the poetry of labor and birth.

If you answer a single prayer,
the muscle of my heart,
still gnarled like hickory,
will animate both my feet
and I will dance again.

A PRAYER ON BEHALF OF THOSE WHO SPEAK IN ORDER TO HEAR THEMSELVES THINK

(Extroverts)

Beloved God of many voices,
act kindly toward my incessant chatter—
those squealing disharmonies
hideously slithering
from out the writhing nest of eels
inside my brain.

Act kindly Beloved,
toward the shambling Tevye of my faith
who listens by nattering
more than stillness in the morning,
more than stillness in the morning.
Did I repeat myself?

Act kindly Beloved,
toward my noisy cohort,
for we are aliens to silence,

stillness,
and prayer.

Act kindly Beloved,
toward our poor untethered lot
who awkwardly look back
over our shoulder into a mirror without reflection.
We are not graceful like the others—
the ones standing egret-like,
peering out from inside their elegant
introverted stillness.

Act kindly Beloved,
and cast no aspersions
or any cruel tease upon us,
for we are those who speak in order to listen.

Enter our words instead—even just some of them—
enter as a meteor hurtling to earth in flames,
to explode and crackle,
to unleash crisp sounds of unexpected light.
Turn us into electric confabulations,
stunning those around us
with our unexpected wisdom

and astonishing our own emptiness
with strange and unbegotten substance.

We will hear you if you do Beloved,
but it is noisy in here,
so speak up
and speak often.

Amen.   Amen.   Amen.

Essay: "God"

Here is what I want you to know about God...

...I wouldn't leave you hanging.

But honestly, you didn't think I had any special knowledge about God did you, just because I am a preacher and have been preaching for four decades? Let me tell you what we learned about in seminary.

Theology is the academic study of doctrines— -- what institutionally acceptable theologians think about the Bible, pronouncing who and what has authority to speak for God, how many angels are dancing on the head of a pin and who can see them, and other such absurdities. It is ridiculous considering that no one knows God and never has; no one.

I hope that is not bitter news to you. It shouldn't be; it says so right at the very beginning of the Bible. If you go along with reputable Biblical scholars and recognize that the Book of Genesis was created long after the Book of Exodus, then Moses and the burning bush is right there at the beginning.

The thing to know about Genesis is that it was created after Exodus because they needed a back story—as in some smart kid in class asked, "Well where did Moses come from? What was happening with God and the world before Moses?" Genesis filled in those holes.

Allow me to backtrack a moment. By reputable Biblical scholars, I mean those who seek to understand first meanings, and do not allow any particular church doctrine to get in the way of their scholarship and its outcome. They want to know as much as possible, the origins of the who, what, when, and where of each verse. They use archeology, anthropology, linguistic analysis, textual criticism, scientific dating methods, and an array of tools to hear the text as it was spoken during its generation—when possible.

Okay, now I can go on.

When Moses first encounters God, and God tells him to go back to Egypt and set his people free, Moses quite rightfully wants to know which God is speaking to him. He wants to know what kind of weapons this god has, because if he is going to go back to Egypt where there is a price on his head for murder, and go up against Pharaoh who was also a god, Moses wants to know what this God in the burning bush has going for him.

So, Moses asks God's name, because knowing the name of anything is to know its power. To know the name of a god is to know what kind of power that god has.

This God tells Moses "I will be who I will be." In other words, shut up. You don't get to know my name. As far as power is concerned, I am God—The God.

Moses, perhaps the greatest prophet of all time (although Islam and Christianity would argue with that), doesn't get to know who or what God is. No one does. But most of the rest of the Bible, and certainly the two millennia of Christianity, were spent trying to define God once and for all, and for all people. It is absurd and ridiculous.

Nothing is what I know about God. God is mystical presence occasionally seen reflected through awe and gratitude, and a presence now and again experienced in the midst of community, flowing through the veins of pain, joy, and love. Oddly, that is enough for me.

Short Story: "The Conversation"

The minister, hunching his large frame through the aisle of first class, toward the humble section, looked at his ticket and peered ahead, past the curtain separating his section from the one he was stopped in. Someone far ahead of him held up the line as she tried to stuff a bag that wouldn't fit into the overhead. This was in the first decade of the present century, before electronic tickets and penalized baggage checks, or an up-charge for a seat in the Emergency Exit row.

He could feel sweat forming on his brow and moisture under his arms from the long walk in the airport and the cramped air of the parked airplane. It was likely also his anxiety about flying, and the cross-country flight with five hours of dooms-day thoughts ahead. But immediately he was relieved to discover the front aisle seat in the second-class section was empty on this airline that didn't have assigned seating. An Emergency Exit seat no less. In those days, the first row Emergency Exit had nearly five feet of leg room. He started to hum.

He placed his bulky coat above and kept a small carrier bag with him as he sat down. Withdrawing a laptop from the bag, and pushing the bag under the seat, he leaned back and relaxed. Still humming quietly to himself, the words of Mick Jagger's and

Keith Richard's, "You can't always get what you want" wiggled around in his head.

It was a Saturday morning and he had to preach the next day, so his plan was to write the sermon within the ample flight time before him. With plenty of legroom, his plan was unfolding nicely. Now the conundrum. The Sunday morning reading from the prophet Jeremiah was staring him in the face and demanding he explain about the prophets. The general public thinks that prophets are people who predict the future when in fact they have more to say about the meaning of the present. But whenever he started talking about such things he could almost watch the attention of the congregation slump in the pews.

Immediately he was distracted. Next to him was a young woman who never looked up from the papers she was reading when he sat down. Next to her was a man in his late thirties with graying sideburns who was also reading.

As soon as the minister sat down and buckled his seatbelt, the young woman began chatting. She was a Financial Analyst, she told him, with an international brokerage house on her way to a two-year posting in Amsterdam. Within minutes the minister learned she was Chinese American, in her late-twenties, and had been adopted by an American couple when she was six.

She was a Chatty Cathy doll wound tightly and talking non-stop—anxiety-driven the pastor noted to himself. She introduced the minister to the man in the window seat. He was unrelated to the woman, a Frenchman now living in the United States after marrying an American. He seemed eager to chat as well.

The sermon hung over the minister's head and he felt his fingers wanting to open the computer on his lap. The attendant whispered in his ear from behind and asked him to put it away until the captain indicated it was okay to lower the seat trays (even though he had no seat tray in his aisle). Meanwhile, his two aisle mates animatedly conversed next to him. The woman between him and the Frenchman acted as host, peppering each of them with relentless questions. Inevitably she asked the question he was dreading.

When a stranger asked him what he did, his answer would produce either discomfort or embarrassment. Magically, he must somehow know the person didn't go to church last Sunday or stole a cookie from the cookie jar, or alternatively, it produced an immediate silence and a hurried exit from the topic and an end to the conversation. Occasionally, it evoked an inappropriate sense of solidarity as the stranger gleefully assumed that meant they shared all the same beliefs and prejudices.

But these two companions created a new category. The woman,

a bundle of fearless energy, responded, "Oh, that means you do not believe in evolution!"

Before he could respond to her, she launched into her autobiography.

"My American Mom and Dad are Christian. But I cannot be Christian," she said, "because I cannot believe in all that they believe."

She cataloged a long list of her parent's beliefs that she could not believe, which told the minister it was an Evangelical megachurch. She talked at great length about having to attend the theologically conservative and doctrinaire congregation even though she could not believe in "any of those things."

"Well, I don't believe in those things either," the minister retorted.

"What? How can you be Christian and not believe?"

"I don't see any conflict between the poetic descriptions of creation in Genesis and the more observable ideas of evolution," the minister said.

She laughed and laughed. "How can you be Christian and

believe in Evolution?"

She was totally flabbergasted at what seemed to be an entirely new category of thought. It seemed to the minister that being religious to her was so completely alien that she could be utterly unselfconscious and talk about beliefs cherished by millions in the same way she would talk about liking or disliking Nike or Reebok.

She went on to confide to the minister that she thought her American parent's church had the same cult of personality as the Chinese Cultural Revolution had with Mao and his successors. They were utterly decadent, she scowled, while at the same time punishing and impoverishing others for straying from the Party Line. Without irony in her expression, she told him the cult around Mao was also a religion.

The Frenchman was less complex.

"I don't believe any of that stuff," he sniffed.

"You know, don't you, that spirituality is not the same thing as religion, and it is possible to embrace the idea of God without endorsing the beliefs with which Christianity, Judaism, or Islam define God?" The Minister began.

"What do you mean," the Frenchman asked.

"Well, religion is to spirituality as educational institutions are to learning. You can become an educated person on your own without going to school, but it is a lot harder as you often have to re-invent the wheel along the way."

They both looked confused.

"Religion is the practice of spirituality, and Christianity is only one of the great historic spiritual practices. It is a choice which one we practice—not a requirement as in the cult of personality."

"Why did you choose Christianity if you believe in Evolution and you don't believe Jesus is God," the woman asked with a bit of exasperation tossed in.

"I was a philosophy major in college. I began with an emphasis in historic Chinese philosophy in fact. While I grew up in a church, by the time I was in college I didn't think I believed in God anymore. I was certain I wasn't a Christian."

"What happened? A conversion like my parents?" She asked, clearly annoyed and expecting him to preach at her.

"First, I thought it was a choice. Then, after a few years of studying, I realized I am a Christian by culture, regardless of whether I want to be or not. I could study Buddhism, but I would be a Westernized Buddhist. I would be a capitalist American bringing my consumeristic culture with me into whatever religion I practiced and it would change the pristine ideas I was studying. In the same way that American Christianity has radically changed European Christianity, and European Christianity had utterly changed the Semitic nature of the fledgling religion that emerged from Judah and Galilee, and along the Mediterranean. So, I decided to study and try to understand Christianity before becoming something else. And then it stuck."

"But what good is it?" The Frenchman asked point blank.

"What good is what?"

"What good is spirituality? What good does it do for you?"

"If our spiritual practice is motivated by getting something in return for it, then it isn't good for anything."

"No," the woman jumped in. "My parents say they get Salvation from taking Jesus as their personal Lord and Savior. They say they get cleansed from their sins if they believe these things the preacher preaches."

"I know, but that is not the spirituality I practice. If we practice spirituality to get something, it will likely do just the opposite." Then the minister got a little excited, even emphatic. "What good does it do to listen to music? What good does it do to see paintings or sculpture? What good does it do to dance?"

Both of his aisle mates looked confused.

The minister thought for a moment and then he grabbed his bag from under the seat, ruffled around and pulled out a piece of notebook paper. With the tip of his pen, he poked a tiny hole in the middle of the piece of paper.

"See this hole?" He held it up to his eye and looked at them through it. "This is how much of the cosmos we can see."

When he took the paper down the Frenchman was looking back at him with a wrinkled brow and pursed lips. *What?* was written all over his face.

"With all of our scientific knowledge," the minister continued, pausing to look for a moment directly at the woman, "and with all of our historical perspectives, and with all of our technological advances, we still only have a peephole through which to view all that is out there, right?"

Both the Frenchman and the Chinese American woman agreed.

"So, practicing spirituality makes the hole a little bigger." He stopped and smiled. "There is more than one way of knowing, right? I mean, the more ways we have of knowing and seeing, the bigger our peephole."

"So, what does that get us," he asked rhetorically. "Maybe nothing. But maybe it allows us to be wiser. Maybe we get to be more perceptive, and maybe that gives us a chance to be less reactive in life, moving more gracefully with the currents we cannot see but we can feel. Maybe—"

"Maybe," the woman interrupted, "I could be your kind of Christian." And then she laughed and laughed.

Then the minister lost his restraint. He couldn't help himself. He had lost all sense of self-consciousness about dumping on people that may not want to hear what he thought. It was as if all the voices trapped inside suddenly were finding a way out.

"Here is the point," he smiled. "There are people who make the peephole bigger for us. They are called "prophets" in Judaism, Christianity, and Islam. They voice God the way that a piano voices music. The prophet isn't the music itself, but he or she delivers the sound. There have always been prophets. Famous ones whose names we know—Moses, Amos, Deborah, Micah, Isaiah—and not so famous ones that are only known to a few."

He stopped and looked at them intently. The woman was still looking at him with an interested look on her face while the Frenchman was staring out the window.

"We humans are herd animals, you know," he said toward the woman. "We think we are great individuals, like roving Grizzly bears, but really, we are pack animals. We are easily shaped by media-generated perceptions and other purveyors of inculturation—ones we prize, like great classical literature, and ones we may disparage, like pornography and racism.

"We are herded by people who wield instruments of power and influence. We like to think there is someone who really knows the right answer and has the ability to guide us into safety and security. And that desire is easily manipulated. When a critical mass of people responds affirmatively to a suggestion, then the herd moves as a group."

"I'm not a herd animal," the Frenchman snorted.

"I am not, maybe maybe…" the woman said quietly.

"I don't mean to suggest that 'herdness' is wrong or sinful or stupid, it is just what we are, and it is better to understand who and what we are and account for it, than it is to be in denial of it and more easily manipulated."

The Frenchman turned back toward the window while the young woman bent her head down seemingly in thought—at least that is what the minister hoped. He was afraid he may have offended them, or worse, bored them. He wasn't used to talking religion—or spirituality—with strangers. Most of the time, he was even uncomfortable having such a conversation with people he knew.

He considered not saying anything else, and finally opening his laptop to write his sermon, but it felt like the conversation needed a conclusion. As he was wondering what to do the woman spoke up.

"You mentioned 'prophets.' I have heard the preacher in my American parent's church quote prophets, but I never paid attention. Who are they and what do they do?"

"Prophets break the herd," the minister said without hesitation. He had been jolted into action by her unexpected inquiry.

"Somehow, they say things that are hard to hear, in such a way that we can hear them, so that we suddenly see the place we have been standing in an entirely new light. It is as if suddenly we see our own living room with the furniture all moved around, and it gives us an entirely new perspective. The prophet gives us new eyes like that, and for a moment we can see we have been herded and where we are heading and the hazard of continuing to go there."

"Does that make sense?" He added after a pause. "We may get annoyed at the prophet for pushing us to see what we do not want to see. And if the prophet is effective at opening our eyes and getting under our skin—and begins to threaten business-as-usual for those who profit most from business-as-usual—well then, we might decide the prophet needs to leave."

The young woman grew silent as the Frenchman already had. The minister felt his face turn hot and red, he imagined. That familiar old embarrassment had returned, and he knew he had said more than he should have—they hadn't asked him for a sermon after all. He opened his laptop.

The rest of the flight was quiet, the Frenchman sleeping most of the way and looking out the window otherwise. The young woman read papers in her notebook and then buried her nose, almost literally, in a Stephen King novel.

Before the minister was able to finish writing his sermon, the pilot announced they were getting ready to land. The minister had been so wrapped up in his one-sided conversation with the young woman and Frenchman, and then in remorse for having gone so far down the road with them, that he had forgotten to get anxious. He smiled at the thought.

When they landed, the young woman and Frenchman talked about the flight connections they had to make and how much time they had to make them. The minister backed up in the aisle to allow the young woman and Frenchman to depart first since he had no connection to make. They said polite goodbyes with smiles and joined in the quiet single-file line through First Class and out the Jetway into the terminal. They both disappeared into the non-stop stream of travelers moving within the concourse as if currents in a river.

The minister stopped to pull on his coat when a woman's voice behind him said, "Excuse me, sir."

He turned around to see a fashionably dressed woman who looked to be in her forties. He did not recognize her at all and found himself straightening up as if meeting someone important.

"I wanted to thank you for that conversation," she said with a smile. "I was on the aisle seat in the last row in First Class just in front of you. What you told those folks at the beginning of the flight—I was entirely entertained and stimulated. They didn't seem that interested, but I would have loved to hear you say more. Thank you so much." She reached her hand forward and shook his, then also joined the river of people moving in both directions.

The minister stood there a moment with a dumb expression on his face, only slowly moving into the concourse, trying to understand what had just taken place. Finally, there was nothing else to do but make his way to the baggage area.

Awed

by the Ordinary Sacred

Essay: "Autumn"

My neighbor's black-eyed Susans are still vibrant. Their round black eyes are bigger now, bulging out from yellow faces. But that chroma of yellow! No human concocted hue comes close to that screaming lemon-mango-egg yolk-citrine gift of Mother Nature.

Thankfully, our lavender and verbena are popping purple in this newly ordained Mum season, but the writing is on the wall for gardens everywhere. Our flowers are on hospice care.

The Autumnal Equinox arrives here at three twenty-one p.m. today. But we knew it was happening before it was announced, didn't we?

One day, back in August, something told us the fingers of autumn were reaching into the bale of summer. A certain touch of wind, a scent, the color of a leaf, a flock of birds, maybe even a shadow cast at the wrong time of day. Though we had our summer clothes on and were soaking up the joy that the hot season brings, there was an ever-so-slight knock on the door.

Our bodies get us ready before we enter any season, even before we are cognizant of its arrival. It takes ten to twenty days to adjust from one season to the next, so 62 degrees in early autumn feels chilly even though in early April it feels like a feast of warmth. This is homeostasis, the brain regulating the body to maintain our equilibrium.

While our skin is the receptor, our brain is the barometer regulating blood flow, sweat glands, and heart rate as the seasons change around us. Right now, with autumn arriving, our blood vessels are constricting ever so slightly to preserve heat. The brain sets our thermostat to preserve the core temperature of our bodies. Homeostasis.

Homeostasis is our body's ability to maintain a fairly constant internal temperature and biological environment even though external changes are taking place all around us. Our brains use feedback from what's going on in the atmosphere to adjust our biology to compensate for those changes. While we may feel vulnerable to potential attacks from COVID, cancer, or Lime disease, it is amazing how well our body is regulated and is able to adjust to the massive seasonal changes on Earth.

Autumnal nostalgia is a real thing upon which the commercial drive for pumpkin, pumpkin spice, and Halloween depends on. It is deeply ingrained in our olfactory nerves. Higher temperatures in summer heighten the number of smells our noses receive, while cooler temperatures diminish the quantity and complexity of the odors around us. Thus, the cooler temperatures of autumn empty the stage for the aromas of Fall to dominate. They have less competition, and we associate them with this time of year.

Dying leaves exhale their last breath and collectively fill the air with gases, just like ozone is released from the soil after a good rain. There are thousands and millions dying all around us. Their crunching bodies beneath our shoes crackle the decay of lives lost. The scent of all that death, moist and fragrant in the soil, cleaves to our memories—a lifetime of memories. Everything we remember from the autumns in our childhood, youth, and longer is a ghostly presence annealed to the scents of decay. Hayrides, bonfires, candy apples, and football games, all attached to the aromas of autumn. Take a moment to stop and appreciate how amazing it all is.

I WONDER

Nancy came to mind
    in between hip flexion
        and pelvic tilting—
mandatory floor mechanics
to relieve an old back
and strengthen a sagging core.

I pray for her in the dark
on a latex mattress with liminal mind
posing toward sleep.
There are those few
for whom I promised prayer
and lately have kept my word.

I wonder why I wondered about her?

Should I text each face
I wonder about
when I wonder about her
or him?

       Would that be
a kind of prayer,
I wonder?

I wonder how someone would feel,
knowing they were in the wet
of my mind?
Would they like it?
Feel afraid?
Shudder?
Would I, I wonder,
be discomforted to know
       I entered a mind,
someone else's mind?

No.

INVERSE WISDOM

   Suffocate, I will,
if the clouds don't disperse soon
and reveal a naked sun
in a field of blue.

It's November, or is it
December? Maybe even January.
But still, we deserve
life without a ceiling.

I deserve life without a ceiling.

What? You say it's not about
fairness but the weather?
I take it personally—this
is an abomination.

I want, I insist, I demand
at least one full day with sunshine
every week

from now until Groundhogs Day.

It is my right.

TWO POETS WRITING

She stood behind me,
a presence.
Her words written
three thousand miles from here.
Her breath
the only sound
when she stood
writing poetry
with words
intertwined with mine.

This is how
two minds
reside
together
in
one
space

at
one
time

apart.

TO THE POEM SURGEONS

Provoked by critics of Mary Oliver's poetry in the shadow of her death

Facing surgery:
I read about it online—WebMD and Cleveland Clinic.
A little knowledge is a dangerous thing
and that is all I have.

My investments are diving
below the line on spidery Stock Market charts.
I tune into the experts on Bloomberg;
They speak a language I do not understand.

To the poets I turn.
I read them, sneering back and forth
about lines, and words, and rhythms
and I simply do not understand.
The poems they skewer, I do understand.

The world has become too big.
Too complex.

Too ornery.

Too much for specializing

and not enough for living.

I understand.

To the surgeon I hope knows everything

he or she needs to know, I surrender my body.

To Vanguard and Fidelity, I give permission

to risk my future this much, but no more.

To the poets and scholars of poetry,

I give nothing.

Your words about my words are not sacred.

WHEN I AM DEAD AND GONE

—To those I love

When I am dead and gone
what will they say?

When I am dead and gone,
I will be dead and gone.
Whatever they say
will soon enough go unsaid—
and forgotten.
There comes a time
after the needle has no more wax to travel—
when the record keeps spinning
but the music ends. Just gone
as if it never was.

When I am on my deathbed,
stuck sharing a room
bathed in snarling florescence
and the pungent scents of nursing home,
or bedridden with a nurse's aide

cleaning my privates
while family can't quite look away,
will I have enough mind left to ask the question,
and will I care what they say
about my life?

Regrets are okay.
They just mean I was brave enough
    to risk failure
and gritty enough
to acknowledge it.

Shame can't be helped.
It was a poisonous pill
sewn into the lining of my stomach
early on.

Grief, well that just means I loved.

Hmm. In the aging cellar of my life
amidst the regret, shame, and grief
I want to feel
I used what was given
with vigor

with courage

with ingenuity

even with wisdom

right up to the end.

I want them to look at the wagon tracks behind me,
note whatever I accomplished
and whoever I was able to touch
and love,
and then say out loud, "He's got nothing left in the tank."

I want them to believe
everything I had
was given up
to something bigger than me.

Or maybe, I want them to say,
"That man met his calling alright,
and God must have grinned
a great big 'Boy Howdy'
when he reached the pearly gates."

Or maybe I just want everyone left,
whose toes are still wiggling in the sand

when my final wave
leaves the shore,

to know I loved them.

YOGI FRIEND

Sandy

I've written this for your voice:
the way it curls around the leg of a word,
tonguing it with exact precision:
sweet-like, with
an upward lilt
but also, sometimes, an elongation…

THE COLORS!

>—A reflection on someone else's COVID experience

Quarantined

from myself, fighting

for breath,

frozen in place,

flat on my back,

staring up at the trees overhead

alone...

away from others

    and cut off from myself.

I was vacuum-packed

in misery—sensory deprivation. Then

somehow...a breath.

Deep from within,

a breath

moved from below, slowly,

all the way up, it

parted my lips.

The colors did it.

It was the colors, the vibrant
lucid colors...
perspicuous sky blue
limpid leaf red—no orange,
no fire.

Miraculously powerful,
    they pulled a breath up from within
my constricted body, pinched
as it was by an isolation,
so terrible it threatened
my life.
The colors did that.
The colors released me.

Published with gratitude to Tracy Genovese

MOONLIGHT SONATA AND AUGUST RAIN

Hear now, the sound of drops plinging
on the edges of steel,
then rolling down as small rivulets
between the ridges of the metal roof.
Dog shakes at my feet
'neath a sound-carpet
echoing harshly within her more tender ears.

Enter Ludwig's notes—
invisibly culled by lithe fingers,
sweeping and stroking ivory,
a polyrhythm of sound
to the Almighty's tongue
showering the earth
with a wet kiss.
This gift of new sound
soothes the dog,
but I hold them both—the righteous rain
and Ludwig— between my ears
and am grateful.

Essay: "Snow Thief"

I was going to write about America falling apart at the seams, but then it snowed.

Snow can be magical, even as it can be overwhelming, dangerous, and disruptive. A big snow means a day of digging out and snuggling in.

Rabia could sense it early Monday morning. She could only see outside from one spot in the house, and when she saw what she had been sensing, a kind of quiver emanated from the inside out.

I was excited too. I hadn't used my battery powered snow blower in a couple of years, not since we moved into our little net-zero solar home. We downsized the yard as well as the size of the house, so most tools and implements were sold off or given away. But I kept that snow blower. Anyone with a snow blower loves to power sweep their own walks and then venture out clearing the neighbor's walks too. It's a unique kind of fun, or if not quite fun, satisfaction. My back being what it is these days, shoveling is out of the question, but snow blower? Sure.

I arose early to see what Mother Nature had delivered. Tiptoeing to the door (but not really, I don't tip toe anymore) as if down the stairs on Christmas morning to see the tree with presents under it, I saw the snow through the glass. Rabia was next to me wagging her tail. Immediately I was confused.

The section of the porch between the sidewalk and door seemed clear. *Wind? Is it drifting badly?* I wondered.

The battery had been charged the night before and sat by the door ready to go. On with the big Muck boots that cover and warm from ankle almost to knee. On with the long coat because the blowing-snow cakes on everything. Knit Carhartt hat over my ears and Turtleneck-sleeve below my chin. Gloves in hand, I opened the door to enter magic.

What? A cleared walk? It was not yet seven in the morning, and someone had shoveled my walk. Not only mine but those to the left and to the right.

It has been since my twenties that I have tracked an animal, but snow makes it fairly easy. I was going to solve this crime. There were boot prints in the snow moving south. I was on the case: A secret snow thief had shoveled all the walks on my small street. Rising very early, even before this would-be snow thief did, the mystery shoveler had come and gone with stealth.

Hmm, even before I got to the end of the boot prints, I could see they stopped at a sidewalk five or six houses away. Oh, wait, he's there shoveling his own walk! Stop thief! You took my snow away!

I had found the culprit, a doctor no less. With only his intrepid shovel by his side, he manhandled the snow away. Just to be kind, he shoveled the walks of his neighbors even before the light of day. How could I write about America falling apart at the seams when I awoke to that? And then, of course, there was Rabia who pranced and danced and ran crazy-eights in the snow.

THE GOD WHO EATS BLACK HOLES FOR A SNACK

—A sermonic poem for The Transfiguration

Begrudgingly,
with a limp and wobble,
I walk while Rabia trots,
sniffs, and wags.
I sigh, harrumph,
and shuffle
while she delicately
circles the right spot
to do one, then the other,
of the thing
we walk for.

One thing
we do together
is sit on "our" bench
by the lake.
Me,

because I am
a sedentary contemplator;
Her,
because I rub her belly.

The sun
was brilliant,
already a ragged ball of flames
hovering
only inches
above the water.
A ribbon of gold
unrolled toward us
on white shouldered waves,
pushed by a stiff south wind
from Watkins Glen.

Sometimes,
when we are sitting there,
I pray.

Sometimes I talk,
Tevia style,
to the Creator-Of-All-That-Is, letting God know

what I think should be done
as if divinity
was a power at my command.

Other times,
most of the time,
I sit.
I invite the wind,
the waves,
the sun or clouds,
even rain or snow,
to speak to me
whatever words
I need to hear.

But last Wednesday,
as I raised my head toward
the rising sun,
I could not look up.
I was about to say something
Peter-like about tents
when the intensity of light
refused me.
Mind you, I had sunglasses on.

Still, I could not raise my head
above a Rabia level bow
to speak toward the sun.

I had already decided
intuitively—which
is how I decide most things—
to use the sun
as a surrogate for God.
I was planning to look
toward the sun
and offer prayers.
But the sun
had another idea.
"Down you fool," the sun
might as well have grumbled.
I could not look up.

The sun was too much:
too brilliant,
too intense,
too radiant
for me to look at it
even through dark lenses.

And that, of course,
was perfect.

God
is no manageable deity,
no genie in a bottle
corked for later use.
God is not hiding in a tabernacle,
as in the high churches—
a candle burning
in red glass
to warn that the real Jesus
is there.
God won't play peek-a-boo
from underneath the altar.
No messages in a bottle
sent up through the pages
of the Bible.
No whispering, even
into the ears of preachers
who tell us
what God thinks,
and what God wants,

and what God would have us do.

We do not have
a domesticated God,
served up in bite-size pieces
so we can chew and swallow
our religion safely.

There is no God like that,
not even close.
The Creator-Of-All-That-Is—
eternal,
timeless.
cosmic
—eats Black Holes
for a snack.

The Milky Way,
where our smallish galaxy
of sun and planets
forms a little tail at the end,
holds fifty other galaxies.
The biggest galaxy
in the Milky Way

has a belly filled with ten billion stars
bulging 14,000 light-years in diameter.
Ten billion of our suns!

There was a time so sweet
when we thought there was just one universe.
Remember, not so long ago?
But now we know there are more,
and that just our little universe
carries two hundred billion galaxies
as if they were a mere armload of wood.

God,
our little God,
is the Creator
of all those billions of billions
of galaxies,
each with tens of billions of suns.

God,
our little God,
is *that* God.
And we somehow
have gotten the idea

that we can reduce *that* God
to a manageable size
so that we can know it,
and understand it,
and follow its every command,
and digest it
like some cookie that delights us.

When Moses
came out of the cloud—
probably the small Sagittarius
Star Cloud
known as Messier 24—
he shined.
Moses' face shined
so brightly
that for the rest of his life
he had to wear a veil
over his head.

Moses on his mountain
and Jesus on his mountain
are cartoon stories
that stutter

over ordinary truths
lodged in fantastical memories.

The ordinary truth is
that God is THAT God,
and we are nothing but star dust
gathered in a temporary body.
We can't even get within
three million miles
of our own sun
before burning up.
How close could we get
to THAT God
without obliteration?

The Bible was not a baby
born all at once
in a single dump.
No, it was composed of stories told
before they were written.
Stories told
by storytellers
in circles of hushed voices
and passed down

for years or decades
and even centuries
before written and edited.

Moses and Jesus
on their mountaintops
are shadows of the stories
that were told
to evoke the breadth,
and depth
and power
of a God
they knew better than we know. *That* God.

We think
that because we know
about cells,
about atoms,
about sub-atomic particles
and how to split them
to harness bombs,
that we are big and important.

We think

that because
we know how to capture
the power of the sun
and the wind
and fire,
that we are big and full of wisdom.

We think
that because we can fly
and dive
and sail;
because we can vaccinate
and paint
and build
that we are big and powerful.

We are so mistaken.
We are small.
Infinitesimal.
Vulnerable and
fragile
in the presence
of the universe,
let alone in the presence of

the God of all the universes.

The stories remind us
that the humility we lost
in modernity
is a lens
we need
to find and wear
and what we wish to see clearly.

The early morning sun
reminded me
that the transfiguration
is about *that* God.
Small on my bench,
the ribbon of light,
the shoving waves,
a dog content to sit with me
all pushed me back
and ordered me
to reach out
and put on *that* lens.

Parting (Not Last) Words

Essay: "Words Wiggle and Meaning is Slippery"

Words do not hold still. They wiggle.

Words writhe and squirm, sometimes gushing down the trough of history and splashing over the contemporary moment. For example, in Roman times an "addict" was a debtor given to someone as a slave. Then, a mere four hundred years ago, the same word referred to a disciplined practice or passionate devotion to something. Alcohol, cocaine, and Oxycontin have changed how we use the word.

Or take another word, "awful." Seven hundred years ago, this same word that means something ghastly to us now, meant what it sounds like: Something that inspires awe.

Those who learn a second or third language know the difficulty of translating words. Meaning changes when words transition from one language and culture to another. Think of that reality in regard to the Bible, Declaration of Independence, or Constitution.

There is no single original text from which each book of the Bible was translated; rather, it is garnered from hundreds or even thousands of partial manuscripts in multiple languages. The oldest versions used for translation are from Greek, Aramaic, and Hebrew, but there are literally thousands of scraps of papyrus offering snippets of text, in dozens of ancient languages, all competing to be the "oldest known copy." The Bible is strained through the sieve of history, then translated into more than thirteen hundred modern languages. Every translation, and every generation, changes the meaning of every biblical chapter and verse.

Closer to home, take the word "happiness"—as in "pursuit of happiness." We know it from the Declaration of Independence. Our contemporary notion of happiness has to do with feelings related to personal gratification, or what makes us individually happy. But to the founding generation of American revolutionaries, happiness meant, "that feeling of self-worth and dignity you acquire by contributing to your community and to its civic life", (Justice Anthony Kennedy, 2005). Oops, big difference.

When we take into consideration that the meaning of words do not hold still over time or across languages, then we realize that no document from the past stands still, and there is no possibility of determining original meanings when it comes to an ancient document like the Bible, and no possibility of strict literal interpretation when it comes to the Constitution. Each word and each sentence of heirloom documents is a judgment call—a translation even within the same language.

Meanings wiggle as words age, but they thrash and splash as we translate words from language to language, culture to culture, and generation to generation. Socrates was right when he complained that the written word cannot defend itself against misinterpretation or abuse, which led the most famous sage of them all to shun writing altogether.

I say that, and acknowledge the ghost of truth within it, even though I am a writer and preacher—a professional word weasel. What blows my mind is how carelessly words are spewed these days through social media, emails, and television diatribes. Not only are those words defenseless from being corrupted, misused, abused, and contorted, they will be there for as long as each respective medium survives—in some cases, cast beyond our planet and doomed to travel as endless sound bites in space.

While I clearly do not follow Socrates's sage advice to shun writing, I am awe-filled by the power and vulnerability of words. So much so, I dither about mine like a hen with her chicks. I wish everyone did.

Essay: "Is it a wonderful life?"

A haze of white flakes pelted my face. The temperature was in the teens this Monday morning. Dog and I leaned in against the wind as March roared like a lion with forty mph wind gusts. By mid-morning I could see sun and blue trying to peel away the shroud of gray. They didn't succeed. If the app on my phone is correct, April will be entering like a lion and, hopefully, exiting like a lamb.

This past weekend, the life of an ordinary saint I knew entered the ether, but the impact of her gifts and service will ripple outward for generations to come. Many Genevans knew Joanne Wisor as the former mayor, the second woman to serve the city in that capacity (1996-1999). I knew her as a member and leader of my church community, and a person with great personal strength and faith. But this is not a eulogy.

Joanne's passing, added to this year's struggle to open the gateway to Spring, evokes in me thoughts of ordinary saints and the extraordinary resurrections imbued in April's green renewal. They are connected, of course, just as every one of our bodies holds the residue of actual star dust. Across billions of light-years, the connections between stars and planets, quasars with Earth, and the biological lives scattered across it mostly go unnoticed by those of us who don't study such things. Likewise, the connection between our ordinary lives and how we influence and benefit one another, goes unnoticed by us too.

I cannot tell you exactly how Joanne's life changed the world or anyone in it, but I guarantee you it did. I hesitate to sound like the angel in the movie, "It's a Wonderful Life" but it is true that we never know how our actions influence others around us. Seemingly insignificant encounters or conversations can in fact change the trajectory of lives. Joanne had a big life, probably bigger than she would have contemplated as she served the interests of so many institutions and organizations, not to mention cared for and served so many individuals. Just from the scale of the life she lived, I am guessing the reverberation was greater for her than it is for many of us. But all of us, every single one of us, can be certain our lives have and are influencing the course of history—one part and one life at a time.

That is true for negative impacts as well. When we act with rapacious self-interest because we believe it is a dog-eat-dog world and it's better to not get eaten, we help to create that competition. When we act as if the world is split into blue and red, and assume the only people worth helping or listening to are our color, we help to expand that divide. When we consume with abandon and give no thought to our footprint on the environment, we hasten a more volatile world.

When the world loses an ordinary saint who made many people better, we grieve twice: for the one we loved and for the world they made better. I hope you will join me in thinking about what kind of impact we are having, seen or unseen, on the world around us.

Essay: "The Promise of Our Hope"

I am done with election chatter. I wrote last week's column, a truth I hold, and voted early. Done. Time to move on even though the election and all that hangs on it is still in motion all around us. Mary Oliver, please.

As prolific as she was, and as popular as she is, it is still possible you don't know her. She won the Pulitzer Prize and National Book Award, and there are lines from a few of her poems that millions have memorized as if lyrics from a platinum album. According to the National Endowment of the Arts, between 2012 and 2017, the rate of adult consumption of poetry grew by 76%. Mary Oliver may be a primary engine for that growth.

Anyway, this isn't really about Mary Oliver, rather something she said. Listening to a 2015 radio (NPR) interview from "On Being," I was pulled out of the election morass and returned to a focus I prefer: nature, even human nature.

Responding to a question about her childhood, marred horribly by an abusive father, she said, "It was a very bad childhood—for everybody, every member of the household...and I escaped it, barely, with years of trouble...but I was saved by poetry, and I was saved by the beauty of the world."

From a young age, Oliver went looking in the woods for beauty and then wrote about it. It was the looking and listening, the breathing in and touching the world all around us, as closely as possible, that saved her life and gave us so many wonderful poems. In the same interview she observed profoundly: "Attention is the beginning of devotion."

Getting out of the house, if possible, and turning our attention toward the intricacies at our feet and at the end of our arms, will imbue us with a buoyant spirituality that just keeps rising up through calm and storm, beauty and ugliness, joy and sorrow. For example, as I was walking the dog this morning, I noticed a very large and intensely green grasshopper motionless on the cement. Immediately, a famous line from Oliver's poem about a grasshopper came to me, but hers was about a vibrant summer day and a grasshopper eating sugar out of her hand. At my feet was a testament to winter, to mortality, and relentless change—in spite of temperatures more similar to late September than November.

Reflecting on the dead grasshopper, I was reminded that mortality need not be a fearsome grief all the time. There is beauty in it, along with the sorrow of loss. The grasshopper will be folded into the earth and repurposed—nutrients for the green leaves and green grass it may have once eaten. As Oliver notes more than once, though the thing we are will die, none of the parts that made up our whole will. We know this from physics, everything that dies becomes something else. That very fact is the most beautiful poetry of all.

So, while the election chatter reminds us of the angels and demons of our better and worse natures, nature itself reminds us that both life and change are relentless. What we are will change whether we resist or promote it, and the very mortality of what we love makes up the promise of our hope.

Essay: "A Word Meditation for Thanksgiving"

I have written about this before and had the opportunity to talk about it in a recent public forum. It is about gratitude, and what better time to ponder gratitude than the day before Thanksgiving?

Gratitude is an antidote for more of the things that ail us than Bee Propolis. Imagine an Elon Musk, Jeff Bezos, or Donald Trump driven by deep gratitude? I know, right? It would truly be a different world.

I like to imagine that the economy of God operates by the invisible hand of gratitude rather than greed, as in our economy. Please forgive the theological metaphor; even if you do not believe in God, imagine a human society with an economy that held gratitude as its core value, rather than self-interest. If you can't imagine it, I recommend this exercise—even the ability to imagine such a society has a healing quality.

Gratitude also heals grief. As far as I know, it's the only thing that does. It happens over time, of course, rather than with one big swig. Grief is extraordinarily debilitating, but reaching for and touching gratitude for the person or thing lost will work its way into the grief and mellow it. Little by little the grief will dissipate and allow for memories without pain—or at least tolerable pain. I have no idea how or why gratitude works like that, but it does.

Gratitude is also a gateway to awe. Now there is a word we do not utter much: awe. When was the last time you felt awe? If it has been a while, I am betting you need more gratitude in your diet.

The distance from gratitude to awe is a breath, just a breath. When we feel deep gratitude for something we have encountered, there is a good chance it will inspire us to step back and "behold" it rather than consume it. Consumption leads to satiation, and we smile because we have been pleased. Gratitude leads to awe, and we take a deep breath because we can't believe how fortunate we've been to witness whatever has inspired us. And then you know what happens? We immediately want to share it.

When we see an awesome sunset, we want to share it with someone. When we have the taste of delicious ice cream, we just want to keep eating it.

It is crazy how powerful the effect of gratitude is if we cultivate it. Gratitude is one of the amazing elements of character (it's not really an emotion) that is self-generating. The more we experience it the more of it we have. It requires an opening of the heart and appreciative inquiry of the mind for gratitude to seep in and generate a reservoir inside us.

But gratitude can also be fragile. When we gravitate too easily and too often toward self-satisfaction and happiness-driven pleasure seeking, gratitude will evaporate and leave us with its vacancy. Again, I do not know how or why gratitude works this way, just that it does.

Gratitude is like a prism that reflects colorful beads of light every which way—as such, the dimensions of gratitude seem almost infinite. So, as you sit down to your Thanksgiving meal, may I recommend taking a moment to behold the people and feast before you. Take a deep breath and touch gratitude.

Essay: "The Circle Be Unbroken"

A shout out to Alan! I hope I'm spelling his name correctly.

He is my senior by a number of years, I am guessing, but he is still running...and running...and running. Every day in fact.

You may have seen him sometime along the waterfront, chugging along at his own pace on his way to the flagpole and back. I don't know him, we just met. Nonetheless, I am awed and humbled by him.

There were times during the shutdown and after when I could barely walk twenty yards because of an excruciating back problem. When I progressed enough that I could tolerate the few steps it takes to walk my dog three-hundred feet through the tunnel to the lake, I sometimes saw Alan's silhouette running slow and steady against the blue-water background. Seeing this older gentleman running fiercely against the currents of age, I would curse the wind because I was feeling so battered—or he inspired me to keep moving. Sometimes both happened at the same time.

Shift gears to a recent Sunday afternoon. My younger friend Lisa came through the door in tears. She had been stopped at a train intersection, parked in a line of cars, when she spotted a skunk who had been hit by the train. The poor animal was in shock and struggling for life, a grim and bloody scene. It shook and collapsed, withered and pawed, life draining out of it too slowly for mercy. My friend was wracked by compassion as she watched another creature suffer, even a skunk—a beautiful quality of her character.

Suffering and death happen daily, hourly, even minute by minute, but most of us rarely witness it. Often, creatures endure the struggle alone. Lisa being there, and her tears, honored that unfortunate skunk. Because she was willing to look and behold it in her compassionate heart and mind, even from a distance, she honored it.

Aging, struggling, life, and death are the crucible within which all of us dwell. They are the centripetal forces with which we interact; they cause us to change, grow, or wither. Some become misshapen and cynical inside, like those that publicly laughed and mocked the attack on Mr. Pelosi. Others are tender and host compassion. When we become battered, some will crumple and quickly resign. Others become bitter and recalcitrant. Some will heave a shoulder forward and keep moving, a few will even cast a smile as they do.

Alan smiles as he runs. On a wet nasty, cold, gray Monday morning I saw Alan's unmistakable silhouette chugging up the sidewalk toward dog and me sitting on "our" bench. I had not seen him in a while—watching him reminded me of how far I had come since the shutdown and the most crippling days of my back condition. I smiled with gratitude. Then something unexpected happened. He passed us as we sat on the bench watching him jog, turned around at the entrance to the tunnel, and was beginning to head toward Long Pier. Then he stopped, turned to us and asked, "Are you Cam Miller?" I confessed to it. He took off his glove, shook my hand, and thanked me for my Finger Lakes Times columns. Now, we share a mutual admiration circle.

Then, as we chatted briefly, he said, "I'm a friend of Lisa's." Circle complete.

FUNERAL

A sermonic poem owed to "I have hymns you haven't heard" from Rainer Maria Rilke

I said to the God-Of-All-That-Is:
The music found me:
fingered my insides,
played my nerves like ivories,
pulled my feet up and down,
my head back and forth.

The music found me
and played my heart like a song on the wind.

So now Beloved, overrule the meditations of my heart
    and the words from my mouth
that your presence
your wisdom
your love
    your music be known.

So, then I spoke to those gathered,
the ones
who look down and sniffle,
and the ones who look up
with hope
and expectation, and even
the ones who do not want to hear.
I told them what I know
of the music
we have heard.

I said:
"There is music we haven't heard yet.
Did you know it?

A dragon-footed mystery
in flight above our sight.
Did you know God has music we haven't heard yet?

A swift motion
at the corner of our eyes,
shifting grass with a breath,
altering a nation two continents away.
God has music we haven't heard yet.

Do you hear it?
The music, I mean, can you hear it?

Whatever your religion—
whatever you say you believe or don't believe—
can you hear it? The music?

You, yeah you who eschew religion.
You, who refute anything wacko-mystical, who
scorn what you do not have.
Do you hear it? The music?

The cosmos (God) has music we haven't heard yet.

But we are so deeply arrogant!
This species, this mostly hairless fragile species
of eight billion consumers!
We are wobbling along wagon ruts
of assumptions
about the way things are
and how things work
and what—with our great body of knowledge—
we believe
we know

can and cannot happen.
We imagine
we are making
all the music ourselves, or at least
all the music worth listening to.

But there is music we haven't heard yet.
It doesn't emanate from us.

So, stand back, now.
Make room within
all the things we know for certain.
Make room for what we do not know.
For mystery.

Oh, come on, open the cupboard.
Allow what you don't know
to rise like mist
through the creases in your brain,
and wet the mind
with that strangest of all auras—reverence.

Behold the vast unknowing
through which we live our lives.

Stand back and see
what we can never see:
we do not get to know
the full dimensions of those we love.
Everyone
everyone we know and everyone we ever knew
we only see in part.
Lover, friend, mom, uncle, dog—
anyone we know,
we know only in part.
It is all we ever get—a bone
a piece
a shadow
a narrow beam of light;
our lives, their lives, floating particles
we cannot quite hold or see."

Beloved, you have hymns we haven't heard yet.
Play them now, on my words—make them your words, please.
Help them hear.

"I have music in my soul
you will never hear.

You have lyrics
none of us will ever know.

Touch it, now, there inside
where you live alone.

All of us have a deep reservoir inside
known only to ourselves—
not even fully known by us.
It is where we encounter God
and the vast mysteries within our own lives.
Like an iceberg,
we have far more submerged
than we will ever show.
What we do not know
and will not share
and cannot fathom
should be enough
to raise up reverence."

'Stories!' you object.
'Tell all the stories.
We are crammed full of stories,

every ordinary life afire with stories.'"

    (Yes, a bow to EBB)

"See now, hear now.
Even all the stories—
every moment we know
and can remember—all put altogether,
right here,
right now,
would not come close
to the fullness of our now dead friend.
Nor for any life.

Even these puny, ordinary lives of ours!

We have touched more people
than will ever be known.
And we don't get to know
how far
all those touches,
in all those lives we have touched,
will ripple outward
into the future.

Generations?
Centuries?
We don't know.
God shifting a blade of grass with a breath
alters a nation two continents away—
why not the infinitesimal blade of life
we have lived
within our own nanosecond of years?
Our impact,
yours and mine,
will travel farther
than the bounds of our imagination.
This alone
should cause us to stutter
...to cough with reverence.

I am pleading with your here,
asking you to enter the alcove of reverence
because it mitigates our lack of humility
and opens us to the music in our midst.

Let me whisper it straight
so you hear: Reverence
is the gateway to gratitude,
and gratitude

heals grief. It takes time, of course, but gratitude does heal.

In our shroud of grief,
for each beautiful life snatched
from our arms
with or without warning, reverence can allow
even the smallest ray of gratitude
to seep underneath and enter within.
If we can make a little room
in our grief—
push the edges of the shroud
out just a little,
then raise the flap even an inch
so that gratitude enters,
we can touch it.

Eventually, the presence
of gratitude
will help us rise up and out,
lifting ourselves from the most debilitating parts of grief.
Besides, it just feels good
to touch gratitude.

So, did you hear it?

Do you know?
God has music we haven't heard yet.
Amen."

And so, that is what I said
and all I know.

Adapted from sermons in thanksgiving for the lives of all those I have buried.

Acknowledgment

Miller, Cameron. "Parable." Le Mon Juste 2020, Just Poets. Foothills Publishing, USA: 38. Print.

Miller, Cameron. "mercy." *Le Mon Juste 2021*, Just Poets. Foothills Publishing, USA: 2021. 20. Print

Miller, Cameron. "Two poets writing." *Le Mon Juste 2022*, Just Poets. Foothills Publishing, USA: 60. Print.

Miller, Cameron. "To the Poem Surgeons." *Le Mon Juste 2023*, Just Poets. Foothills Publishing, USA: Print.

"Psst. Your Pet Doesn't Know Your Name," "Acts of Love," "Slap me," "Autumn," "Snow Thief," "Words Wiggle and Meaning is Slippery," "Is it a Wonderful Life?,," "The Promise of our Hope," "A Word Meditation for Thanksgiving," "The Circle Be Unbroken," appeared as columns in the series, "Denim Spirit" in *The Finger Lakes Times* (NY) and subsequently as posts on *www.subversivepreacher.org*.

The Back Story

Why mix forms like this, a chaos of essays, poems, and short stories? Because they belong together, just as drama and music belong together in Opera and Musicals. Real life doesn't fit neatly into a single form of narrative. Poetry, essay, and short story, like different genres of music and theater, are ways of sensing, intuiting, forming, and creating, but they need not to be oppositional. The goal of each is to offer the reader an experience of what the writer sees, hears, or feels from different perspectives. The hope is that the reader will suddenly be taken up into the memory of their own life experience, and be compelled to ponder. Just as a painting can pull us in if we allow it, and if it is compelling enough to do so, my desire is to pull you into my experience in order to evoke your own. At that moment, it is then up to you whether or not you enter it, and what you do with it. Isn't that the essence of art?

Spirituality requires all dimensions of the mind: the reasonable as well as the intuitive; the imaginative with the concrete; the visual in addition to the logical. Most of us are not equally adept in all areas, but we need to be practiced in each. A mind of pure reason is a crippled intellect that has poor vision, and a purely fanciful mind is childish. These are all valuable capacities for being human, and they work better in conjunction with one another rather than in isolation. Thus, these poems, essays, and short stories are intermingled in hopes of pushing, cajoling, and tripping the reader into the various modes of the mind. If you are a spiritually-minded person, I hope these essays and poems will chAlange your spirituality. If you are agnostic, then I hope they will provoke an opening to the mystical reality others of us experience.

To paraphrase a Jesus saying, where we pick apart the bones of our experience wisdom will arise. It is how we come to understand ourselves and allow our understanding to move us outward. Piece by piece, bit by bit, reflecting on our experiences can move us beyond ourselves in concentric circles to apprehend others, the world, and ever-so-slightly, God.

About the Author

Cameron Miller is the author of three novels, a collection of poetry, numerous poems published in anthologies, and now a memoir in poetry and prose. Born in Indiana and having served congregations in Ohio, Massachusetts, Vermont, and New York, he is now settled in the Finger Lakes. The arc of Miller's writing follows his discernment of the sacred in the midst of the ordinary without using religious or theological language to do so. Whether in his weekly newspaper column, sermons and podcasts published on www.subversivepreacher.org, or in his poetry and prose in print, he seeks to tease out the voices and presence of the holy where most people don't go looking for it.

Available from the publisher or where books are sold: "Last Will & Testament, A Memoir in Poetry and Prose" (Unsolicited Press, December 2024); "Cairn, poems and essays" (Unsolicited Press, 2020); "Thoughtwall Cafe, Espresso for the Third Season of Life" (Unsolicited Press, 2018); "The Steam Room Diaries" (Tumbleweed Books, 2015).